Mindfulness

Beginners Guide on How to Shut Off Your Brain and Stay in the Moment

Free membership into the Mastermind Self Development Group!

For a limited time, you can join the Mastermind Self Development Group for free! You will receive videos and articles from top authorities in self development as well as a special group only offers on new books and training programs. There will also be a monthly member only draw that gives you a chance to win any book from your Kindle wish list!

If you sign up through this link http://www.mastermindselfdevelopment.com/specialreport you will also get a special free report on the Wheel of Life. This report will give you a visual look at your current life and then take you through a series of exercises that will help you plan what your perfect life looks like. The workbook does not end there; we then take you through a process to help you plan how to achieve that perfect life. The process is very powerful and has the potential to change your life forever. Join the group now and start to change your life!
http://www.mastermindselfdevelopment.com/specialreport

Table of Contents

Introduction

Chapter 1: The Value of Mindfulness

Chapter 2: Creating the Calm

Chapter 3: Peace in Pandemonium

Chapter 4: The Practical Practice

Chapter 5: Maintaining Mindfulness

Conclusion

Introduction

Thank you and congratulations on purchasing this book! "*Mindfulness:* Beginners Guide on How to Shut Off Your Brain and Stay in the Moment" is a book written specifically for individuals who want to become more mindful, but who have a hard time encouraging their brain to be quiet. While you may feel as though mindfulness is not the technique for you, the truth is that everyone who has mastered mindfulness at one point or another had the exact same difficulty!

This book has been carefully crafted to bring resolutions for all who are struggling to achieve mindfulness in their lives. The wording and instructions are created in an easy-to-understand method that will allow you to understand the simplicity of being mindful, and how you can effortlessly draw it into your own life.

Mindfulness is a highly valuable tool that has the ability to achieve many things in a person's life. Whether you are seeking to add value to each day, eliminate the stress of worrying, or improve your quality of life, you can achieve all of that through mindfulness. In this book, you will be guided on how to achieve mindfulness on an average day, even if you are experiencing a particularly large amount of chaos or stress that may be causing you to feel extra edgy.

It is important to remember that mindfulness is a practice. Once you learn how to be mindful, you will have an easy time re-learning it. You will need to make sure you take the time each day to practice mindfulness, even when you become a master at it. Mindfulness is a balancing act where we are continually practicing our ability to stay in tune. Sometimes, you may notice that you have not been practicing mindfulness in your life. The result may show up as added stress, less mental involvement in day to day life, less clarity on what you are doing from moment to moment, and less quality of time spent with those around you. If you notice this is happening, the best thing you can do is become mindful of the existence of the chaos, and allow yourself to realign with a mindful state and start practicing your techniques again. In this book, you are going to learn exactly how you can do that.

Being mindful may feel difficult, especially for beginners. It is not natural in this day and age to tune out from the rest of the world and narrow in on what is happening in the moment. However, once you understand and implement this valuable technique in your life, you will notice that you feel your stress levels reduce significantly. You will also experience life greater, and with more joy. If you are ready to dive into learning about mindfulness, you are ready to begin chapter one.

Chapter 1: The Value of Mindfulness

Throughout history, a huge number of people have practiced mindfulness. As such, we see it across many religions and many other areas of culture. Mindfulness is a simple practice that, when practiced regularly, allows for humans to stay more focused on the specific task at hand, and resist the temptation to worry about or become absorbed in events of the past or the unpredictable future.

Mindfulness is a relatively simple task to learn once you understand exactly what it is and how you can use it in your daily life. This precious technique has the ability to add value to your life in many ways. Those who practice mindfulness on a regular basis notice increased happiness, greater synchronicity with themselves and the world around them, and even health improvements. Mindfulness truly is a valuable technique that has the ability to offer you a number of different benefits.

Emotional Benefits

Many people report a high number of emotional benefits that come from practicing mindfulness in their daily lives, and it makes sense as to why. Being mindful and staying present in the moment allows for people to experience the greatest benefit of each experience in life. Because of this heightened involvement in the experience, people report a greater result from it. The more involved they are in the moment, mentally, the more they understand about the moment and the more value they gain from it. This is because they are not renting any of their mind space out to unnecessary or irrelevant thoughts or emotions for the present moment. They are taking the time to notice every element of the experience, draw in all that it has to offer, and really take a heightened value from it. Because of this, people report feeling more peaceful, less stressed, happier, and a more genuine sense of joy that comes from being mindful.

Look at the below example to gain a greater understanding as to how mindfulness can change a situation:

Situation 1: *Sally was spending time with her Dad, as they often did on Fridays after school. He liked to pick her up and take her out for her favorite treat: ice cream. Sally loved spending the extra time with her Dad, but he always seemed distant. He would regularly check his watch or his phone, and often didn't listen to what hear her at all. Even though she loved having that one-on-one time, she wished her Dad would stop worrying about his work and pay more attention to her.*

Above, you can see that Sally's Dad was not being mindful. His frequent checking of his watch and his phone signified that he was somewhere else in his mind. Sometimes, he was so distant, he didn't even hear her talking! This can be damaging to relationships with other people and can lead to stress, discomfort, anger, and other unnecessary issues between two people. This is not a good state to be in, especially considering Sally is talking about her own Dad!

Situation 2: *Sally was spending time with her Dad, as they often did on Fridays after school. He liked to pick her up and take her out for her favorite treat: ice cream. Sally loved spending extra time with her Dad. He always gave her all of the attention she needed and wanted during this time. He would talk to her about how her day went, ask her how school was doing, and even offer to help her practice more for the cheerleading team! Sally knew he was a busy man because of his demanding job, so she really appreciated that he took the time to put his work aside and give her his full attention for their time together.*

Above, Sally's Dad was being mindful. He was actively involved in the moment, he was listening to his daughter and engaging in meaningful conversation with her. He put away his phone and stopped checking his watch, and he really gave his daughter the quality time that they both needed. This time would nurture their relationship together, and create a more powerful and meaningful bond between the father and daughter, which is valuable for both of them.

Being mindful has the ability to offer a significant number of emotional benefits. The more mindful you are, the more present you are in the moment. This makes your experiences much more valuable and can help bring you more joy, a greater sense of connection, reduced stress, and greater fulfillment in life.

Health Benefits

Believe it or not, mindfulness does have actual physical health benefits. The more mindful you are in life, the healthier you are going to be. While this phenomenal technique isn't so powerful that it can cure ailments, it does have the ability to prevent and reduce the occurrence of a number of symptoms and diseases. There's a very practical and logical reason as to why, too.

When you are mindful, you are present in the moment. This translates to a number of different benefits that contribute to the increased quality of health that can be drawn from being a mindful person. First, being more present in the moment means that you are less stressed and agitated. Remember all of the emotional benefits you learned about a moment ago? Someone who is in a less stressed and calmer state of mind is much less likely to experience common symptoms and diseases that are born from stress. These include but are not limited to: high blood pressure; headaches; tense muscles; a sore jaw; and even some cardiac ailments. Stress has the ability to cause a number of different diseases in our body. While becoming less stressed isn't the *only* way to prevent or eliminate these ailments and diseases, it is a great way to reduce your risk of getting them to begin with. It can also assist you in eliminating them when used alongside a qualified health plan set out by your health provider.

In addition to allowing you to eliminate or at least reduce symptoms and diseases, mindfulness can also allow you to be more in sync with your body. When this occurs, you will be much more likely to take care of your body in the way it needs to be taken care of. For example, if you are thirsty, you will drink water. If you are hungry, you will eat. If you are mindful, you are likely going to choose a healthy and fulfilling food option over a sugary-filled quick-fix to your hunger. If you are sleepy, you will go to bed. So on, and so forth. The more mindful you are, the more in sync with your body you will be, and the more likely you will take care of it in a way that keeps it healthy and working optimally. Additionally, if you notice something wrong, you will be able to schedule an appointment with your doctor right away, as opposed to ignoring it for several weeks because you are unaware of it at first.

As you can see, mindfulness has a high number of health benefits, beyond emotional ones. When you are mindful, you reduce your risk of contracting ailments and diseases that can greatly decrease your quality of life, or in extreme cases, kill you. This practice is a wonderful technique to stay in tune with your body, listen to what it needs, and nourish it in ways that allow you to flourish and work in the most optimal way.

Worldly Benefits

If you thought mindfulness only had a benefit on yourself, you were wrong! Mindfulness is a practical and strategic way to benefit the world around you, as well! This amazing technique allows you the opportunity to improve your world through several different ways.

First, when you are mindful, you are much less likely to engage in arguments or conflict with other people. When you do choose to engage in a conflict, you will be much more rational about your approach, and the situation will likely diffuse quickly. If it doesn't, you will recognize that no benefit is being drawn from the experience, and you will remove yourself from the situation. Mindful people are generally much less emotionally charged in a negative format than those who are not mindful. They are more likely to be able to handle anger and stresses strategically, which means that even their "opponent" will end the situation in a more calm and rational way. This may simply diffuse one set of bad emotions, or it could trickle and encourage the other person to go learn about mindfulness and practice being more peaceful and calm in their own lives. You never know!

Additionally, the more we are in sync with the world around us, the more we are going to experience value from the world, and give value to the world. We are more likely to notice people who are struggling, so we can offer help. We are more likely to experience the highest joy we possibly can, which truly is contagious! Many other people who experience your intoxicating joy are going to turn around and experience some of their own as a result!

Finally, people who are mindful are generally a lot more considerate of the Earth itself. They tend to take better care of the world around them through many measures, including but not limited to: recycling, not littering, helping clean up after others, taking care of plants and animals, and more! Doing all of this contributes to the healthy production and growth of the planet, which means that you are assisting it in thriving and maintaining its health!

Being a mindful person adds greater value to life, for the person who is mindful both emotionally and mentally, for the people around them, and for the Earth itself. When people are mindful, they are less stressed and more at peace, they are more engaged with those around them, and they are much more likely to experience greater fulfillment out of their lives. This practice and technique is potentially one of the most valuable ones you could ever teach yourself.

Chapter 2: Creating the Calm

The very first step in becoming more mindful in your life is learning to create the calmness. Or, in other words, learning to relax your mind and let things be. In this chapter, you will learn exactly how you can let go of everything that is stressing you out from your past and your future, and focus strictly on the present moment. This is really the biggest lesson in mindfulness that you need to learn. Once you learn what mindfulness is and how it feels, you will have a much easier time applying it to various situations throughout your life.

Learning to be mindful is truly a process. You are going to start out and probably have a hard time with it at first, and then you are going to continue practicing it until you are a master at it. Once you learn how to become mindful the first time, practicing mindfulness constantly becomes easier every single time you practice it. So, if you ever find you've gone a few days particularly stressed out and lacking mindfulness, you will know exactly what you need to do in order to reclaim your peace through mindfulness.

The first thing is understanding exactly what mindfulness is. Essentially, mindfulness is a form of being present in the moment. It is a time where you prevent yourself from becoming absorbed in thoughts of the past or the perceived future, and you let yourself experience exactly what is materializing right in front of you, right in that moment. So, you are noticing the colors of your surroundings, the smells, the feelings, the tastes if there are any, and the sounds. You really want to enrich as many of your senses with each experience as you possibly can, *and* take the time to actually notice them.

The easiest way to become mindful in a moment is to practice the 5-4-3-2-1 technique. This technique became popular within the last few years for good reason. It is an excellent way to help reclaim your current moment and encourage your mind to focus on what is physically going on around you, rather than straying away into other parts of your mind. In order to practice this method, all you have to do is quietly tell yourself five things you can see, four things you can touch, three things you can hear, two things you can smell and one thing you can taste. This helps you focus on exactly what is happening in the present, and keeps your mind actively paying attention to your current experiences.

You should practice this technique any time you want to become mindful of the moment around you. Observing your experiences with all of your senses is a great way to fully immerse yourself in the present and truly gain all of the value it has to offer. The more you practice this, the easier it will become for you.

You may be wondering when you should use mindfulness. Of course, it's not practical to expect that you are going to be mindful every minute of every day. Even mindfulness masters can't do that, so no matter how long and hard you practice, you are going to experience moments where your mind strays away from you. That is completely normal and absolutely okay. The human brain is a natural wanderer and part of being mindful and experiencing life as fully as possible is recognizing that and giving your brain the permission to do so. The goal is not to have you constantly having to stop your brain from doing what it naturally wants to do. Instead, it's controlling your brain to not wander when the situation warrants for you to be present. When you are working, when you are waking up, when you are eating something new, when you are spending time with people you love, and many other situations are more fully experienced when you practice mindfulness while doing so. However, that's not to say that you can never allow your mind to wander. In this short list below, you will learn more techniques about mindfulness and when you should apply this strategy in your life.

Give Yourself Mind Permission to Wander

Since your mind naturally wants to wander, sometimes the best way to become mindful is to let your mind wander. This may sound counterproductive, but the reality is that it will actually save and enhance your mindfulness practice. When your mind wants to wander and you're consistently having to tell it no, you are not going to be practicing mindfulness because you will instead be having an internal conflict with your mind. Rather than allowing that to go on and then stressing yourself out further, you can simply give yourself permission to let your mind wander. You can let it go for a set period of time, say like five minutes, and then when that time is up, you can gently bring your mind back to the present moment and carry on with your mindfulness practice. This sounds like a paradox, but sometimes being mindful of your desire to let your mind wander is the best way to do it!

Practice Mindfulness During Regular Routines

Often times, our regular routines become mundane and repetitive. We do them so often that we no longer think about what we're doing, we just do it. You may notice this to be the case for many instances in your day and life, for example: brushing your teeth, driving to work, large portions of your work day, coming home from work, making supper, and more. These are all a great time to practice being mindful. When we tend to "check out" for these activities, we can stop feeling present in the moment and start working on autopilot. Not only does this detract from mindfulness, but it can actually lead to your emotional run-down, and sometimes even dangerous situations, such as if you are on mental autopilot while driving to work. These are some of the best times to practice being mindful. You may find that your routine is a lot more fun than you were experiencing, or that there are new and more efficient ways you could be doing things!

Switch It Up!

If you are feeling that your life is too full of routines, another great way to practice mindfulness and really gain a lot of value from it is to switch up your routines! If you always wake up, stretch, go to the bathroom, turn on the coffee pot and then flick on the morning news, then try something else for a change! Wake up, go to the bathroom, set the kettle to boil and make yourself a nice beverage and then drink it on the balcony! You may choose to take a different route to work, walk a different way to your office, sit down in a different way, or do any number of different things to help switch up the pace of things. When you break the routine, you give your mind a bit of a break from the autopilot mode and you encourage it to pay attention by making it interested in what is going on. Sometimes becoming mindful of your routine and during your routines will actually lead you to make changes because you will realize you have been doing unnecessary extras, or that certain things aren't as efficient or effective anymore. Being mindful and giving yourself permission to switch it up is a great way to get your brain active in your daily routines again and give it a break from the regular day-to-day activities that can become boring and mundane.

Practice Mindfulness as Soon as You Wake

When we wake up, many of us don't jump straight out of bed. Even if you do, it is still a great time to practice mindfulness. Since you have been asleep for a while, you have been on somewhat of a mental vacation from your body. During this time, your brain has been wandering for several hours, typically. So, this is a great time to practice mindfulness! See if you can notice the light shining in through the window, the sensation of the blankets or the air on your skin, the sound of the birds or of other people in your home, and any smells and tastes you may notice.

The morning is a great time to practice mindfulness because it allows you to start your day off with being more aware of your surroundings. They say that when we start our day out a certain way, it can make it easier to carry on that task throughout the rest of the day. With that logic, if you are mindfulness first thing in the morning, you will likely find it much easier to be mindful throughout the rest of your day. It is a great way to set the tone, have a positive morning, and really create the perfect setting to allow the rest of your day to be mindful and peaceful.

Short and Sweet Wins the Treat

Remember how you learned that mindfulness isn't something that you are expected to, or even capable of, practicing for every minute of the day? If you struggle with mindfulness, sometimes it's easiest just to be mindful in short bursts. In fact, science has proven that if you are mindful for short periods several times during the day as opposed to one single longer period, you will gain greater benefit from it. With that knowledge, it is a good idea to allow yourself to become present for a few minutes at a time throughout your entire day, instead of expecting yourself to become mindful about everything you do all of the time, or only practicing it once a day for lengthy time frames. Being mindful doesn't have to be a long and hard technique that you put a significant amount of effort into for several hours each day. Instead, draw your mind in when you remember to, and practice doing it more and more each day.

Practice Mindfulness When You're Waiting

When we are waiting for things, we tend to become stressed out, bored, or even agitated. Most humans do not like to wait, which means that this is a great time for you to practice mindfulness! Instead of letting your mind wander down the rabbit hole of negativity that leads you to feel uncomfortable and upset about a situation that you can't control, practice being calm and peaceful. Notice the other people in the lineup, recognize that you're all waiting together, listen to the sounds around you, see what else you can notice about the particular situation. You will be surprised at how enjoyable it can be to stop and observe those around us during these periods where we're forced to wait. You can even do this if you're waiting to be taken off of hold on the phone, when you're waiting for an appointment in a lobby, or at any other time that you find yourself waiting around. It is a great chance to regroup and reframe an otherwise bland, or even stressful activity!

Assign a Reminder Prompt to Help You

Many people find it extremely helpful to associate something with mindfulness and use it as an opportunity to remind themselves to be mindful. There are many ways you may do this in your life, and how you personally choose to do it will be unique to you. However, it can be extremely beneficial to have something that you associate with mindfulness that will prompt you to practice mindfulness throughout your day. Some people choose something simple such as a bracelet or a certain trinket they carry around in their pocket, so that any time they touch, see or notice the item, they are reminded to practice mindfulness. In this day and age, we are also granted with the gift of technology. If you find having a trinket around with you doesn't remind you to stay mindful, you may prefer to set reminders in your phone or switch your phone background to something that will prompt you to practice mindfulness throughout the day. However, you choose to do it, having these prompts are a great way to remember to practice mindfulness and infuse it into your everyday life. Again, you don't have to practice mindfulness constantly, but practicing it in short bursts several times throughout the day is an excellent way to increase the value you gain from mindfulness, emotionally, physically, and otherwise.

Practice Meditation

Meditation is essentially a prolonged practice of mindfulness. Many people love using meditation as a means to infuse an even higher quality of mindfulness into their daily routines. Meditation is an excellent opportunity to objectively explore the thoughts in your mind and guide yourself to a new state of calm. This is especially helpful if you feel that something has been bugging you for a while. Meditation may seem difficult, especially to a beginner, but it is actually quite simple. In order to practice meditation, all you need to do is give yourself a set amount of time, set a timer on your phone if you need to, and then close your eyes and release your control over your mind. Every time you notice your mind has wandered "too far", you can gently practice bringing it back to the center. Some choose to hold an image in their mind, and when their thoughts wander, at any time that they've noticed it's happened, they gently bring their mind back to the thought of the image. You may find that your mind wanders a lot, or that it can be hard to even realize that it has done so. This is completely natural, and you will experience this for the majority of your meditation practices, even when you become a master at it. The best thing you can do is give yourself the permission to practice meditation without judging yourself for how you do so.

The Conclusion

Mindfulness is an ongoing practice that you will learn about as you continue to practice the techniques you have been provided with here. You may realize that it is hard at first, but in time you will get much better at it. Remember, there are going to be times that you struggle with mindfulness, even when you are a master. The best way to keep yourself on the path of mindfulness is to set reminders and encourage yourself to practice mindfulness, especially during mundane and routine activities that we generally set ourselves to "autopilot" for us to complete. You will likely find that the more you practice, the easier it is to remember to do so. Like other skills, mindfulness is one you will master if you practice it often enough. This way, if you ever find that you have gone a prolonged period of time without mindfulness, it will be easy to draw it back into your life and pick up where you left off. This practice is not meant to be a stressful one or one that you worry about having to learn. Instead, it is one that will help you learn more about yourself and the world around you, while in turn providing you with significant benefits related to your health, your emotions, your mental wellbeing, and even the world around you.

Chapter 3: Peace in Pandemonium

There is one specific time when you may want to practice mindfulness, but you are having a difficult time. This is one of the hardest points to master mindfulness, and once you do so, you'll know that you are mindfulness master. The hardest time to practice and maintain mindfulness is when you are experiencing any form of conflict. Whether your conflict is internal with yourself, external with another human, or external with the environment you're in, conflict can create a great difficulty when it comes to practicing mindfulness. Consequently, it is one of the best times to practice mindfulness, as well.

The moment you notice you are in a situation that involves conflict, regardless of what type of conflict, you are going to want to use your learned practice to infuse mindfulness into the situation. This is going to quickly allow you to rationalize your emotions, adjust your action, and likely diffuse the situation quickly. You will enable yourself and that which you are in conflict with the gift of being respected and appreciated as it is, free of judgment. You allow yourself the permission to recognize the situation, honor your discomfort, and respond in such a way that allows all parties to be at peace with the resolution. Mindfulness during conflict is one of the most powerful ways to turn a difficult situation into something easier to manage. You are about to learn exactly how you can practice mindfulness during a difficult or conflicting situation, and how it is going to benefit your life in many ways beyond what simple daily mindfulness can do on its own.

The following acronym "RAIN" is a great skill to practice when you are experiencing conflict. This simple acronym will allow you to regain your mindfulness practice and use it as a means to eliminate the conflict you are currently experiencing. When you practice this, you will likely find that at first that it can be difficult. After you become used to using it, however, you will probably find that it becomes easier, or even second nature whenever you are being faced with conflict. The simplicity of this acronym makes it easy to remember, even during a hard situation, and can help you quickly diffuse the situation at hand.

Recognize the Conflict

The first and most important part of practicing mindfulness during conflict is recognizing that the conflict is occurring. You are likely not going to have the time or desire to practice the 5-4-3-2-1 strategy, as conflict is usually fast and heated. Instead, simply take the time to recognize the conflict. You should then give yourself a moment to become aware of your personal sensations. What are you feeling in your body and in your mind? What emotions are you bringing into this experience that may be making it harder for you to be rational? You may want to form judgments around these thoughts or feelings or try and ignore them because they are unpleasant, but the reality is that you need to recognize them, and the best way to do so is to eliminate judgment and simply just recognize as much as you can.

Once you recognize your thoughts and emotions, as well as physical experiences, it will be easier to give them a label. Often when we are in conflict, the only emotion we feel we are experiencing is anger. Generally, that is not the case. We are instead feeling a number of emotions, or one particularly strong emotion that is uncomfortable and often mislabeled as anger. It could be jealousy, hurt, sadness, worry, or any other number of emotions. Recognizing the exact emotions that you experience will give you the opportunity to address them appropriately. It also gives you an opportunity to have a greater awareness of yourself, and potentially learn some important things about yourself that you may not have learned about otherwise.

Allow Yourself (and Others) To Own Their Opinion

Once you have recognized the situation, your personal sensations and emotions, and the particular underlying emotion or emotions that you are experiencing, you need to practice "allowing". This means that you are just allowing life to be. You allow yourself to have your right to your opinion, and you allow others to do the same. You should allow yourself to have the experience of the negative emotions, even if it hurts, and allow yourself to learn from what the emotions are trying to teach you. A great way to give yourself permission to allow things to happen as they are is to mentally say "yes" to your emotions. Allow yourself to accept your emotions as they are, and allow them to be experienced fully. Doing this is going to give you the opportunity to quickly and completely address the emotions in the situation, rather than bottling them up and drawing them out later at an equally destructive time.

Investigate the Situation

Sometimes when you recognize the situation and allow the emotions to be felt and allow yourself to simply experience life, you will feel the conflict quickly fade. Other times, it may persist. If you are experiencing a type of conflict that is particularly persistent and you are having a hard time managing it, you may want to move on to the step called "investigate". This gives you the ability to further explore the situation and grow from it. The following questions are a great way to help yourself address emotions, especially if you are not sure exactly what you are feeling, as well as address the situation, especially if you are not sure of exactly what has happened:

1. "What is the tone of the experience?" (Negative, neutral, or positive)
2. "What specific event triggered this conflict?"
3. "What about this event made it triggering to me?"
4. "Have there been similar events in the past that triggered me before?"
5. "What is the story that I am telling myself about these particular feelings?"
6. "What is the story that these particular feelings are trying to tell me?"
7. "Are there any alternative stories that exist for these feelings I am experiencing?"
8. "Is the story I am telling myself actually realistic?"
9. "Do I have any bodily sensations connected to this particular experience?"

The more you investigate, the more you are going to learn from the situation. You will often find surprising and interesting answers that help draw you deeper into your own existence and understand why certain things make you feel certain ways, especially if they seem to be a trend. This will allow you to become more mindful of the conflict itself, but will also allow you to become more mindful of you as a person and how you can nurture yourself in a way that will reduce or eliminate these conflicts going forward.

If you are having a hard time discovering the emotional attachments to the conflict, or are unsure as to why they are affecting you, it can be a good idea to address these with a series of investigation questions. This will allow you to gain greater clarity on the situation and respond in a better way in the future.

Non-Identification from the Situation

While this step is not a step that you take action on, it is one that is involved in the conflict-resolution process when using mindfulness. You will know you have successfully used mindfulness in your conflicting situation when you are no longer identifying with the situation. Instead of saying things like "why me?" or "what did I do to deserve this?", you will be in a position where you understand the conflict and recognize it was simply a difficult situation. Your perspective will be shifted, and you will notice that you no longer identify with the situation and that you instead recognize it for what it is, allow it to be, and carry on.

Mindfulness can be particularly hard when you are in a conflicting situation. It can be easy to become immersed in the feelings you are experiencing and feed into them, whether they are ones of sadness, anger, hurt, or other difficult emotions. When we feel these, we tend to ignore *why* and focus more on eliminating them through action. That is why we often associate yelling, screaming, temper tantrums, and other negative elimination actions with these emotions. The more we get stuck in our heads and fail to address the situation in a mindful manner, the deeper it seeds into our bodies and makes it harder for us to respond in any other way. That is why it is crucial that you practice mindfulness, especially during conflicting situations.

Added Health Benefits of Mindfulness During Conflict

As mentioned previously, there are added benefits of practicing mindfulness during conflicting situations. These benefits are largely related to mental health and have a lasting value in our lives. The first way mindfulness during conflict benefits you is that it essentially trains your brain to react in a more peaceful and rational way with certain triggers. This allows your brain to learn new patterns that will make it easier for you to act with mindfulness in future conflicting situations. The more you practice mindfulness during conflict, the easier it will become!

The second way that mindfulness helps during conflict is by allowing you to address your internal experiences related to specific triggers. This gives you the ability to look deeper within' yourself and truly understand why things are difficult for you. The more you practice understanding your conflicts on this deeper level, the more you are going to understand yourself and the greater your mindfulness practice will be. It will also give you the ability to work through residual triggers and make it easier for you to eliminate those triggers altogether, so you won't have to worry about them coming up for you anymore!

You are halfway done!

Congratulations on making it to the halfway point of the journey. Many try and give up long before even getting to this point, so you are to be congratulated on this. You have shown that you are serious about getting better every day. I am also serious about improving my life, and helping others get better along the way. To do this I need your feedback. Click on the link below and take a moment to let me know how this book has helped you. If you feel there is something missing or something you would like to see differently, I would love to know about it. I want to ensure that as you and I improve, this book continues to improve as well. Thank you for taking the time to ensure that we are all getting the most from each other.

Chapter 4: The Practical Practice

Despite what you have already learned, there are many more ways still to practice mindfulness in your life. The more practical the application is, the easier it will be to practice and the more you are going to learn from it. For some people, setting aside time to practice mindfulness every day is simply not something they are willing to do. While it can be beneficial to do so, there are other even more practical ways to infuse mindfulness into your day, should you decide you prefer to do it that way.

In this chapter, we are going to further explore the practicality of mindfulness, and how you can use it in your day to day life. These simple moments in your life are a great time to practice mindfulness and really draw the best value from it that you possibly can. When you are practicing mindfulness, you may wish to start with a very practical application, then gradually increase the amount of time you spend practicing this habit. Whichever way you choose to do it, it is completely up to you!

Be Mindful When You Eat

Many of us are in such a rush that when we eat, we plow through our meals as quickly as we can. The experience of food has been largely lost on us, especially in modern times where fast-paced life and fast-paced food are the norm. One of the best times you can introduce mindfulness into your day is while you are eating. Being mindful when you eat is an incredible way to turn eating into a pleasurable experience. You will learn what exactly you like and what you don't like, you will give yourself the chance to thoroughly taste the foods you are eating, and you will allow yourself the opportunity to truly enjoy the experience of eating. As well, when you are full, you will recognize that and stop eating, which means you will always feel satisfied and fulfilled after a meal, instead of overfull or uncomfortable. Many people who choose to eat mindfully find that they stay away from foods that are distasteful and unhealthy, like fast foods, and start to enjoy more quality foods, as well.

You don't have to reserve mindfulness for the process of eating, alone, either. You can also practice mindfulness when you are cooking. Take time to observe all of the colors and scents coming together, notice the way the food looks as it becomes closer and closer to being completed. The more you invest in being mindful during your eating experience, the more enjoyable eating is going to be. A great reason to practice mindfulness during your meals is that in doing so, you will spend more time paying attention to your body. That way, when you are full, you will finish. You may notice you become full much sooner than you'd previously thought. This is a great way to stay healthy and allow your body the opportunity to take a break once it's done. Many people who eat mindfully find that they no longer gorge themselves on meals and that they enjoy themselves a lot more. Cooking and eating are a great opportunity to practice mindfulness and truly experience the joy and satisfaction that food has to offer when it is appreciated appropriately.

When You're Dwelling On the Past

Virtually everyone spends time thinking about the past, and at one time or another, we've all caught ourselves dwelling on it. The past is something that can be a valuable learning tool, but it can also detract from our present and future if we start to dwell on it. Many people stop using the past as a learning experience and start using it as a punishment to keep themselves from repeating things they did in the past that caused pain in their lives. What this does is harm them every single time they decide to invest more of their valuable time and emotion into this thought. The best thing you can do when this is happening is become mindful.

Being mindful about your past, particularly when you are dwelling on it, means that you will spend time recognizing that it is in the past. Instead of using it as a weapon against yourself or a punishment, you will start to use it as an opportunity to learn and grow. You will recognize why it hurt you, and what has made you cling on to that experience for so long. You will also have the opportunity to learn how you get through difficult times, and how they can assist you with growth. It won't necessarily make it easier to overcome future internal conflicts, but it will definitely give you a blueprint to effectively get there.

While Driving

Many people these days spend a great deal of time in our cars. Unfortunately, a lot of people also become so used to driving that they are no longer mindful of the experience itself. This is why many accidents happen: people become what we like to call "over confident" and they get into an accident. In other words, they became so used to driving that they stopped paying as much attention and respecting the danger that coincides with driving. A great way to change this up is to practice mindfulness while you are driving. When you are driving, you can practice mindfulness by spending more time noticing what is around you, paying attention to your mirrors, and watching your speed. You can take a few deep breaths when you're at stoplights and regroup yourself. Sometimes, a great way to enhance your mindfulness when driving is to turn off the music and really pay attention to the moment around you. This change in the familiar sound that fills your car can really help trigger you to become more mindful. Using time spent driving in your car is a great opportunity to practice mindfulness, as well as eliminate the "overconfidence" factor that can be a major risk when people are too comfortable with their driving patterns and routines.

When You Arrive at Work

So many people arrive at work and immediately become stressed out. In fact, they become stressed out on their way to work. This stress is often not provoked by anything aside from simply arriving at work. For many people, the workplace is an emotional trigger to experience stress or some other uncomfortable emotion. A great opportunity for practicing mindfulness is when you first arrive at work. Take time to notice how you are feeling, and what sort of physical sensations are attached to those feelings. Then, you can also take the time to consider why those feelings occur, and how they are truly affecting your day-to-day life. The reality is, many of us, if not all of us, have to work and keep our jobs. Since that is a factor we cannot change, it is not valuable to allow it to cause us significant stress and internal turmoil each day. Instead, you can address these emotions and practice mindfulness to allow yourself to realistically perceive the experience and draw more enjoyment out of your working experiences.

On Your Work Break

Another great time to ground yourself is when you're taking a break at work. This mindfulness experience allows you to regroup from any stress that your work may have caused up until that point, and then start working again with a new, more peaceful frame of mind. Being mindful at work is very important because this is where many of us tend to draw stress from. The more you are able to become mindful of your experiences, shift your focus and perspective, and learn to enjoy your working experience, the less stressful the workplace is going to become for you. A great way to do this is on your breaks.

Alternatively, if you are having a particularly stressful day, it can be beneficial to take a short unscheduled break to practice mindfulness. You can do this in a simple two-minute trip to the washroom. All you need to do is head into the bathroom, and start practicing your mindfulness. You can use the 5-4-3-2-1 method to ground yourself and keep yourself in the present moment. In the process, it will let you take a second to regroup and shift your focus to something more positive that is associated with your work. This is a great way to relieve sudden and urgent stressors that can arise while we are at work.

It is a really good idea to spend a few minutes out of your work day focusing on mindfulness. This is the perfect opportunity to quickly relieve ourselves from stressful emotions and thoughts and allow ourselves to become present in the moment and remember the bigger picture. Doing this will make your workplace less stressful, and help make arriving at work a more enjoyable experience for you.

Grounding Yourself with Noise

We all hear a lot of noise during the day: phones ringing, doorbells chiming, the sounds of cars going by, and so many other sounds. These are all a great opportunity to practice mindfulness. When you are busy with something, you may notice that these sounds all sort of drop to the background and are no longer something you recognize. You should take the opportunity to recognize these sounds whenever you can, and allow yourself to use them as a prompt to quickly ground yourself. Bring yourself back into the present moment, recognize what is going on around you, and become mindful of your current situation. Most often, this is a great way to alleviate stress and become more present each day. You can use this when you are working, when you are at home, or at any other time during your day when you are preoccupied with your thoughts and want to become more focused on the present moment and the world around you.

Leaving Work

Due to many people working jobs, the workplace truly becomes a great opportunity for practicing mindfulness. Perhaps one of the things that makes this the best place is because it is also the place that most people associate with high-stress levels. This may be because the workplace is a place where we all feel pressure to attend in order to maintain our lifestyles, but many of us are not passionate about our jobs. It can lead to a very mundane, boring, and unhappy experience for many people who are going to work. Even if you don't totally dislike your job or have any particular experiences there that cause you to be able to pinpoint your stress to any one thing, it can still become an unhappy place if you are not inspired by it and passionate about the work you are doing.

Practicing mindfulness is a great way to change that. Since you are already practicing when you arrive and when you are on breaks, it makes sense that another great time to practice mindfulness is when you leave work. Doing this gives you the amazing opportunity of leaving behind the days' stressors and appreciating the current moment. At the moment you leave, you no longer have to worry about work duties until you come back. With that knowledge, you should spend time each day practicing mindfulness and leaving your work stressors behind so you can arrive home with a fresh state of mind. Doing this will make your home time much less stressful and more rejuvenating, making it easier to arrive at work the next time you are scheduled to do so.

Arriving Home from A Day Out

Another excellent time to practice mindfulness is when you arrive back home after being away for some time. You may be away due to work, shopping, a trip away, or any other number of things. Regardless of the reason, this is a great opportunity to practice mindfulness. Take a moment to notice the comfort of your home, the familiar surroundings around you, the people or animals that are there to greet you, and anything else that makes you feel comfortable. Do whatever you can to become even more immersed in the current moment. You may choose to diffuse essential oils, brew yourself a luxurious beverage, turn on some of your favorite music, or do any other number of things that will make the experience more peaceful and comforting. These activities will also help draw your awareness to the present situation, making it even more enjoyable for you.

The more you associate your home with peace, comfort, and calmness, the easier it will be to remain mindful when you are home. This is important because you want your home to be a space that is comfortable and safe for you. You should not feel like you have to compensate for difficult emotions or situations when you are in your home. Instead, it should feel like a sanctuary that allows you the opportunity to relieve yourself of the stressors of the external world, and truly enjoy your present moment.

There are many times that you can practice being mindfulness in practical applications. For some people, these opportunities for practicing mindfulness are the best ones, because they allow you to be the most present without having to go out of your way to do so. You do not have to use prompts or "sit on the sidelines" for any given period of time to be mindful. Instead, you simply allow yourself the chance to become mindful at routine moments and turn it into an enjoyable practice that you look forward to on a daily basis. It should be a chance to regroup and recover from anything that may be drawing your attention out and causing stress in your daily life.

Chapter 5: Maintaining Mindfulness

Mindfulness is something that we must practice, constantly. It is not something we achieve ones and maintain forever. Rather, it is something that we must practice on a daily basis in order to maintain. Knowing this, you may find it sometimes is harder to maintain your state of mindfulness than it is for other times. Allow this to bring you peace, knowing that falling out of tune is completely normal. Additionally, the more you fall out of tune and regain your mindfulness, the easier it will be to regain it in the future.

Sometimes, it may be days or even weeks before you notice that you have fallen out of the routine of mindfulness. When you are brand new to the practice, it is easy to forget that you are working to be more mindful in your life. It is not uncommon for people to be extremely mindful for the first several days, and then just completely forget about it. Or, they may even become worn out. Sometimes, being mindful really forces us to confront emotional triggers that we are not interested in confronting. This can make it feel difficult to maintain and may make you feel like it is more comfortable to be ignorant than it is to be mindful. Realize that it is completely normal to run into these blocks, even for the most mindful people you will ever meet.

There are many ways you can contribute to maintaining your mindfulness, several of which we have already explored and discussed in this book. However, it is important to realize that it won't always be easy to maintain your mindfulness. As you've already learned, when there is chaos or confrontation, or when you are experiencing pandemonium, it can be difficult to maintain your mindfulness.

However, sometimes it's just difficult in general. When you are not already wired to a mindful state, it can be hard to remember to stay mindful. Sometimes, you might struggle to remember to do it, not just during hard times, but at any time, because you are not used to it. You may find that you don't realize you haven't been mindful until after the situation has already passed, and then feel guilty or regretful that you didn't do it differently.

There are several things you should realize and do if this occurs, which will help you maintain a mindful state, even if it's sometimes difficult to remember. Below, we are going to explore the various stages of regaining mindfulness, even when you are forgetful or hardwired to respond to situations in a different way.

Give Yourself Permission to Go Slow

Changes don't happen overnight, especially when you are talking about changes for things that you have been doing for many years, perhaps even your whole life. There are no magic formulas, genies or spells that you can use to help you instantaneously become a more mindful person. Instead, you will have to work towards being mindful every day of your life, even once you've already mastered the art of mindfulness.

It is important that you give yourself permission to go as slow as you need to. You are not going to be able to respond to every single situation with mindfulness just because you've decided that's what you want to do. Instead, you are going to find that you will actually rarely respond with mindfulness at first, and that may be very frustrating for you. Realize that you will need to take your time and respect your need to go slow and take this as a learning process. The changes that last the longest are the ones that can take the longest to create. The more effort you have to put in to get yourself into a changed state of mind, the more likely that state will last you. Even if you have to maintain it.

It may take you several weeks, maybe even months to become mindful. Some people even take years to master it. You never know how long it will take you, because of all of the different elements that go into being mindful. Your unique blocks and resistances, lifestyle, and existing level of mindfulness, plus many other things will all contribute to how quickly you can become mindful the majority of the time.

Start Recognizing Triggers

The very first step to switching over to *mindfulness* as your new full-time lifestyle is recognizing triggers. If you are having a hard time maintaining your mindfulness practice because of forgetfulness or a later realization that you "could have" responded with mindfulness, it may be because you are not recognizing your triggers. Take some time and start realizing what your triggers are. These will change on a regular basis, just like life does, so you will need to consistently maintain a check-in process where you recognize what your triggers are and learn why they cause you to respond in certain ways. The more you understand this, the easier it will be for you to maintain mindfulness.

It is not beneficial to judge your triggers. Doing this can cause you to create new blocks and resistances which may further drive you away from a mindful state. Instead, you simply want to recognize what they are. This is an opportunity for you to look deeper within yourself and work on it. At first, there is nothing more that you need to do other than to simply recognize these triggers. Remember, changes don't happen overnight. Instead, you are going to need to take your time. Once you recognize these triggers, practice recognizing them in action. Every time a trigger of yours occurs, recognize it has happened and allow yourself to experience it. Don't encourage any changes yet, just recognize these triggers in action. You will need to practice recognizing new triggers every time one occurs in your life, which is why it is such an important step in maintaining your mindfulness practice.

Create Your Ideal Response

Once you recognize your new triggers and are very confident in your ability to become mindful about them as they are actively happening, you are ready to create your ideal response. You may have already been thinking of an ideal response up until now, but now is the time to think of a practical, mindful and realistic response that you could use when these triggers arise. This should represent your ideal method of how you would want to respond to a trigger.

For example, let's imagine that a particular person makes you angry when you are speaking to them. It gets to the point that you no longer have to hear anything from them at all for you to become angry. Rather, you just become angry from seeing them in general! In this instance, it may seem like the person is the trigger. However, it is likely something that this person has done, said or expressed in the past that has created the trigger. This, in turn, led to a situation where every time you see this person, you think about that experience.

Your ideal response may be that every time you see this person, you feel no emotions at all. You don't necessarily need to feel good or better when you see them. You just need to eliminate the uncomfortable and charged emotions, like anger and hurt. Knowing this, you may set the intention that every time you see this person, you will no longer feel emotionally charged. Instead, you will just feel neutral.

The above situation and correlating ideal response system can be applied to virtually any trigger you experience in life. Once you recognize the trigger and understand when it is actively happening, you'll likely start gaining more information about *why* it happens when you are in that specific situation. Knowing that, you can create an ideal response on how you would rather feel and respond to the situation, versus how you are actively responding. Make sure that the ideal response is something realistic and achievable. Setting the bar too high may prevent you from achieving it at all.

Use Your Ideal Response at Least 25% Of The Time

Again, you need to be prepared to move slowly. You cannot expect that just because you have recognized the trigger and set the intention that you will now respond perfectly every single time. That in itself just isn't realistic. Instead, you should be prepared to respond your ideal way at least 25% of the time. This allows you the opportunity to prepare to respond that way, but also gives you immediate permission that if the situation doesn't go as you desire for it to go, it won't be a "failure" on your part. Rather, it is just one of the 75% of instances where mindfulness hasn't taken root yet!

When you notice the trigger, think about your ideal response. The first several times, you may only think about the response and how you may have made it work in that situation. Eventually, you will arrive at a situation where the ideal response feels like it naturally wants to take place from you. This is the time where you can start practicing it. The more you practice it, the easier it will become for you.

It is important to understand that this is a major part of maintaining mindfulness. Sometimes, you may put in all of the effort to eliminate a trigger, only for it to come back again. If you notice a trigger has fully come back to you, you will need to revert back to this step and practice integrating your ideal response. You may even need to adjust your ideal response to be something more appropriate and fitting so that it is easier for you to respond to it.

Realize that this part of the process takes a long time. It may even take you a long time just to get to the 25% mark. Again, give yourself the chance to take as much time as you need, and don't hold judgment for yourself or the situation when you need time. Giving yourself this permission is the best way to make sure that you don't feel as though you are failing, and that you allow yourself to respond in the most comfortable way. Believe it or not, the more you take the pressure off of yourself to act a certain way, the easier it will be for you to act the way you actually want to act. Eventually, it will come extremely naturally.

Practice the 80/20 Rule

Moving to the 80/20 rule is sometimes gradual, but you should keep this rule in mind as your destination point. While it will be difficult to get here right away, eventually this is where you should aim to end up. It is natural that we may experience triggers, even long after we have worked through them and moved on. Sometimes, it's just something that happens. If you can stay mindful at least 80 percent of the time, then you are doing well. More, and you are golden!

Having a rule like the 80/20 rule gives you permission to make mistakes, without having to consider that as a complete failure of your mindfulness practice. It can take off a great deal of stress and pressure, and make it even easier to be mindful the majority of the time. This works even better because it makes you mindful about your mindfulness. That way, on the times you make a mistake, rather than beating yourself up you can take a look at *why* the trigger happened again, and address it. This will give you the best chance of making sure that you can eliminate triggers once and for all.

Watch Deep Rooted Changes Take Place

The longer you practice mindfulness, the deeper it will root itself in your life. Eventually, you will always address things in this method: by recognizing a trigger, addressing it, creating an alternative response, and enforcing that response at least most of the time. Over time, this will be a natural method for you to address virtually everything in your life, and that will ultimately shift you from a life of ignorance towards your troubles and into a life of mindfulness.

Mindfulness is not an overnight practice that can be mastered right away. Instead, you will have to practice and maintain your practice for the rest of your life. It will become much easier in time, but even when you are a master at mindfulness, you may still find there will be times where you struggle to be mindful.

This is because life is ever-changing and we are emotionally charged beings that will sometimes react instead of respond.

However, you will notice in time that many deep-rooted and powerful changes take place in your life that will guide you in the direction of mindfulness. As this practice becomes more natural to you, you will realize that you are mindful at least 80% of the time in your entire life. You may not notice the changes as they are occurring, but one day you will look back and see just how far you have come!

Always Journal About It

If you are not one to recognize changes that happen in your own life, a good way to start recognizing them is to journal about it. The more you journal about your experiences, the more you can analyze them and make changes, as well as see how far you have come. Journaling has many great purposes when it comes to maintaining your mindfulness practice.

First off, when you journal you can truly gain a greater insight as to how far you have come. You will start to see exactly where you were when you started, and where you are now. You will likely notice that your ability to make changes become quicker and quicker the longer that you practice your mindfulness strategies, and also that you are more capable of adapting to harder situations.

Additionally, journaling is a great way to identify triggers, understand your blocks, and really gain a deeper insight as to what you are going through. Then, you can make more mindful and realistic approaches to how you will handle the situation and what you will do about it. Sometimes, writing about it can significantly help you alleviate a good portion of the stress that is associated with any given situation. As well, you may notice certain trends that occur in regards to your triggers or emotions and have a greater idea as to how you can increase the peace and positivity in your life through your mindfulness practices.

Journaling is an important part of making major life changes. It allows you to reflect deeper on what you are going through, track your progress, and empty yourself of many thoughts that may be using up extra space in your mind. Then, you can focus on the positive and powerful things you want to focus on, and you don't have to keep them in your mind taking up valuable real estate.

Respect, Love, and Honor Yourself Anyway

Some people who are practicing mindfulness may find it difficult to keep themselves positive and love themselves through the struggles. This is especially true when triggers are particularly emotional, or for those who are really early into their mindfulness practice. It can be easy to feel like you are failing, doing something wrong, or otherwise not having success in your practice. You may also find it easy to punish yourself or drag yourself down for what you are going through. It is important to realize that this is not beneficial and that it can actually detract from your mindfulness practice.

A major part of being mindful is feeling positive about yourself and your life. While this may not come easily to you, it is something you should focus on working towards. If you struggle with mindfulness for these reasons, one of your first missions should be to identify your triggers that get you feeling down on yourself and work through those first. You need to learn to practice respecting, loving and honoring yourself anyway.

There is nothing more detrimental to your mindfulness practice than being out of love and harmony with yourself. This can cause you to sabotage your ability to be mindful because you will tear yourself down every time you make a mistake. That is why it is crucial to give yourself room to make mistakes and to love yourself anyway. The easier you are on yourself and the less you hold yourself in contempt for your mistakes, the easier it will be for you to practice mindfulness in your life. It is very important that you give yourself space and permission to make mistakes, and that you love yourself anyway. This will allow you to be the most successful you can possibly be in your mindfulness practice.

As you can see, it won't always be easy to be mindful. Especially when you are brand new to the practice. Sometimes, it won't necessarily be chaos or difficult times that make it hard for you to be mindful. Sometimes, you will simply have a hard time remembering to practice this new way of life due to you being used to living life in a different way for so long. The best thing you can do is give yourself time and space, and draw yourself back to your practice whenever you realize you've strayed away. It may take a while to get there, but the more you practice, the more naturally it will come to you and the more successful you will be in your mindfulness.

Conclusion

Mindfulness is a powerful practice that has the ability to change your life in incredible ways. When you are mindful, you may experience better health, better emotional balances, and lower stress levels. You will give yourself the opportunity to relieve yourself from symptoms of stress. You also gain the ability to recognize what causes you discomfort, and practice working through it so that you can avoid experiencing those unpleasant experiences in the future. Of course, conflict cannot be eliminated, but you allow yourself to grow as a person and work through these conflicts more easily.

The practice of mindfulness can be done anywhere: in your car, at work, at home, or even when you're standing in line at the grocery store. You do not have to limit your practice to any one place or experience. As well, you do not need several minutes or hours to devote to a practice of mindfulness. Instead, you can practice it in as little as two minutes, if that is all you have to dedicate. In fact, it is better to practice mindfulness for a short period of times several times over the course of the day than it is to practice one long burst and never do it again for the rest of the day.

I hope that you learned how to use mindfulness in your daily habits and that it will greatly help you in achieving a more peaceful and empowered life. The practical methods in this book were shared in order to teach you how mindfulness works and exactly how you can work it into your busy routine.

If you enjoyed this book, I ask that you please take the time to rate it on Amazon Kindle. Your honest review would be greatly appreciated.

Thank you, and enjoy your mindful life!

Help me improve this book

While I have never met you, if you made it through this book I know that you are the kind of person that is wanting to get better and is willing to take on tough feedback to get to that point. You and I are cut from the same cloth in that respect. I am always looking to get better and I wish to not just improve myself, but also this book. If you have positive feedback, please take the time to leave a review. It will help other find this book and it can help change a life in the same way that it changed yours. If you have constructive feedback, please also leave a review. It will help me better understand what you, the reader, need to make significant improvements in your life. I will take your feedback and use it to improve this book so that it can become more powerful and beneficial to all those who encounter it.

REMEMBER TO JOIN THE GROUP NOW!

If you have not joined the Mastermind Self Development group yet, now is your time! You will receive videos and articles from top authorities in self development as well as a special group only offers on new books and training programs. There will also be a monthly member only draw that gives you a chance to win any book from your Kindle wish list!

If you sign up through this link http://www.mastermindselfdevelopment.com/specialreport you will also get a special free report on the Wheel of Life. This report will give you a visual look at your current life and then take you through a series of exercises that will help you plan what your perfect life looks like. The workbook does not end there; we then take you through a process to help you plan how to achieve that perfect life. The process is very powerful and has the potential to change your life forever. Join the group now and start to change your life!
http://www.mastermindselfdevelopment.com/specialreport

You will also love these other great titles from Mastermind Self Development!

You will want to check out these other great titles Mastermind Self Development. All available in the Kindle store or you can just click on covers below.

getBook.at/learnfrench   myBook.to/learnspanish

getBook.at/learnlanguages   viewBook.at/selflove

You can also find these titles by searching them in the Kindle store on Amazon.

Mindfulness for Beginners

Secrets to Getting Rid of Stress and Staying in the Moment

Free membership into the Mastermind Self Development Group!

For a limited time, you can join the Mastermind Self Development Group for free! You will receive videos and articles from top authorities in self development as well as a special group only offers on new books and training programs. There will also be a monthly member only draw that gives you a chance to win any book from your Kindle wish list!

If you sign up through this link http://www.mastermindselfdevelopment.com/specialreport you will also get a special free report on the Wheel of Life. This report will give you a visual look at your current life and then take you through a series of exercises that will help you plan what your perfect life looks like. The workbook does not end there; we then take you through a process to help you plan how to achieve that perfect life. The process is very powerful and has the potential to change your life forever. Join the group now and start to change your life!

http://www.mastermindselfdevelopment.com/specialreport

© Copyright 2017 By   Mastermind Self Development   All rights reserved.

This document is geared towards providing exact and reliable information in regards to the topic and issue covered. The publication is sold with the idea that the publisher is not required to render accounting, officially permitted, or otherwise, qualified services. If advice is necessary, legal or professional, a practiced individual in the profession should be ordered.

From a Declaration of Principles which was accepted and approved equally by a Committee of the American Bar Association and a Committee of Publishers and Associations.

In no way is it legal to reproduce, duplicate, or transmit any part of this document in either electronic means or in printed format. Recording of this publication is strictly prohibited and any storage of this document is not allowed unless with written permission from the publisher. All rights reserved.

The information provided herein is stated to be truthful and consistent, in that any liability, in terms of inattention or otherwise, by any usage or abuse of any policies, processes, or directions contained within is the solitary and utter responsibility of the recipient reader. Under no circumstances will any legal responsibility or blame be held against the publisher for any reparation, damages, or monetary loss due to the information herein, either directly or indirectly.

Respective authors own all copyrights not held by the publisher.

The information herein is offered for informational purposes solely, and is universal as so. The presentation of the information is without contract or any type of guarantee assurance.

The trademarks that are used are without any consent, and the publication of the trademark is without permission or backing by the trademark owner. All trademarks and brands within this book are for clarifying purposes only and are the owned by the owners themselves, not affiliated with this document.

Table of Contents

Introduction

Chapter 1: The Secret

Chapter 2: Eliminating Stress

Chapter 3: Staying in the Moment

Chapter 4: Easy Application

Chapter 5: Mindfulness Mastery

Conclusion

Introduction

Mindfulness is a powerful practice that can help you transform your life using simple strategies. Although it may seem difficult at first, mindfulness practices can help you take action in eliminating the stress in your life and staying in the moment. When you practice mindfulness, you learn a great deal about self-awareness and personal care. Mindfulness practices are an excellent tool in learning to navigate your inner self and develop a life that is more peaceful and enjoyable.

In this book *Mindfulness for Beginners: Secrets to Getting Rid of Stress and Staying in the Moment*, you are going to learn a series of valuable and practical applications of mindfulness to help you along your journey. This book is specially designed for anyone who is looking to develop a mindfulness practice but who may not have any clue as to where to start. You will learn about what mindfulness is and isn't, why it is so important to have a mindfulness practice, and easy ways you can develop your own.

Whether you have never heard of mindfulness before or you have dabbled in the practices here and there, this book will help you get on track to lead a more stress-free and positive life. Each chapter is created to provide you with the best and most accurate information to help you along your unique journey and create a practice that will help you eliminate your own personal stresses. To get the maximum benefit from this book, please read it at your own pace, the one that feels most comfortable for you. Enjoy.

Chapter 1: The Secret

Many people think mindfulness is a practice only used by religious groups who have several hours a day to meditate and explore their inner selves. The reality is, mindfulness is actually a phenomenal practice that can be used by anyone to create a more stress-free life. People who are mindful have an easier time staying in the moment, are better at letting things roll off their back, and are more likely to have a more positive and peaceful life with a healthier mental and emotional state.

There are many secrets to mastering mindfulness, but first, you are going to learn exactly what mindfulness is and what it isn't.

Mindfulness Is...

Mindfulness is a practice whereby people learn to tune into their inner selves and identify feelings and emotions they experience in relation to internal and external influences. When people learn to tune into themselves, they gain greater insight into who they are, what they are, and how they are. They learn which things make them feel certain ways and the best coping methods for their unique personality type. Since each person is so vastly different from another, mindfulness is a deeply personal practice that will be experienced entirely different from person to person. Although the methods to develop a mindfulness practice and achieve mindfulness states are similar between each person, the ways people act and react to the experiences, emotions, and feelings that arise for them are completely different.

You can witness mindfulness in yourself when you have an experience, and your first reaction is to look into yourself and identify what you are experiencing in relation to your circumstances. For example, say a co-worker takes credit for the work you did, and instead of fighting, the first thing you do is look inside yourself and see what you feel and how you feel. Once you identify these feelings, you take action based on what feels right for you. When experiences are handled in this manner, they are handled in a way that is optimal to everyone involved. If you were to fight, you would likely not accomplish anything other than to show your boss that you tend to get emotionally charged in these situations. You may experience further frustration and embarrassment or other uncomfortable feelings as a result of your reaction. However, if you were to first look inside and identify your emotions and feelings and then approach the situation in a calmer approach based on what felt right for you, the situation would be handled much easier. Your boss would see how calm and collected you were, you would feel much better knowing that you handled the situation with dignity, and the person who lied would not be a greater cause of stress or frustration for you because you would not actively be in an argument with them.

There are many practical situations in life where you would want to have a mindfulness practice on your side. Many of the experiences we have in life we react to without realizing we have reacted. We then experience the aftershocks of the experience, and many times, they can have negative effects on us. When we have a mindfulness practice in place, we are more likely to recognize the situations that trigger these experiences and identify the ways that we can eliminate our reactions to the triggers. Then, we can choose new preferred methods of responding to the situation and adjust our responses to our desired method. After a while of responding instead of reacting, your reaction will change to your desired response. Then, it will feel natural for you to respond in the way that feels better to you and serves you better.

Mindfulness is a practice that assists people in exploring their inner self and the way they experience the world around them. It is a system of strategies that help you develop a mental state that can assist you in identifying who you are, how you respond to the world, and what makes you feel good. When you learn these things, you gain greater control over your life and your emotions as you learn how you can effectively interact with the world in a way that brings you joy and happiness.

Mindfulness Is Not…

Mindfulness is a powerful practice to help you identify triggers and switch up your response method so that you feel better about the way you lead your life. It is not a magic tool that erases triggers and rewrites your reality without any of your assistance. Think of mindfulness as a pencil with an eraser at one end. Using your own guidance, you and the pencil can work together to erase things you dislike. The marks are left on the page, but they fade away. Then, using your guidance, you and the pencil can rewrite something new into that space. Still, the marks remain beneath the new words, but the new words are more prominent and visible as opposed to the old ones. The old ones are no longer important and no longer hold the priority on the page. Now, everything is focused on the new reality that is written onto the page.

Mindfulness is just like a pencil in a way that it is a tool you can use to erase things you dislike and rewrite your reality. Mindfulness is not a magic wand that will erase your reality and rewrite it for you however, without any effort on your behalf. If you do not put effort into your mindfulness practice, it will not thrive and you will not see the benefits from it. You need to realize that mindfulness is not a medicine, antidote, or magical eraser for life. You will still remember the triggers and you will still identify them even long after they have been rewritten; however, they will not affect you in the same way. They will not be as prominent as they once were. Instead, the prominent experience will be your new reality that you have consciously created using mindfulness as a tool and your own efforts as the driving force.

The Secret

The secret to mindfulness is really simple. So simple in fact, that you might think it's not even a secret at all, nor is it all that impressive. The reality is, when you understand this secret and you put it into effect, your mindfulness practice will grow exponentially, and you will reap in all of the benefits that mindfulness has to offer. The secret to mindfulness is to practice regularly. Mindfulness is not something you attain and then never have to work for again. Mindfulness is called a "practice" for a reason. You must practice each day and put in effort to see the results from your practice. The more you put into your practice, the more you will get out.

That being said, you should not feel like you have to practice mindfulness 24/7. Instead, mindfulness should be regarded as a tool that you use when it is needed, to help you lead a more stress-free and positive lifestyle. Whenever you notice you are feeling overwhelmed, unhappy, stressed, frustrated, or otherwise uncomfortable, you can use mindfulness to help you work through those feelings. If you feel as though you are distracted or have left, mindfulness is a great practice to help bring you back into the room and experience life for what it is.

When you learn about the value of mindfulness and start seeing the results in your own life, you will understand how powerful this practice truly is. The more you use it, the more results you will see, and the more you will remember to use it. In the beginning, you may discover that it is hard to be mindful in many of the situations you encounter. This is completely natural, and you will eventually learn to be mindful more frequently. The best thing you can do is remember that mindfulness takes practice and it isn't a magic wand that can solve all of your problems. It is, however, a tool that you can use when necessary to regain control over your life and reduce the amount of stress you experience.

Chapter 2: Eliminating Stress

One of the best benefits of using mindfulness practices is eliminating stress from your life. While it can take some time, especially if stress is embedded in many areas of your life, the more you practice mindfulness, the easier it will be for you to eliminate the impact that stress has on your life. You will never completely remove stress from your life, but you will be able to alter the way it affects you and how you choose to respond to stress. You can choose to see stress as the end-all-be-all that turns your life upside down, or you can use it as a trigger that informs you that you need to be mindful and change your ways.

There are many techniques you can use to reduce and eliminate stress in your life using mindfulness strategies. The way you choose to do this practice will be entirely up to you and what feels right for you. Generally, most people follow a similar outline but use different specific practices to help them eliminate the stress. The reason why there are so many unique practices is because the way people respond, react, and cope towards different things varies. It is important that you choose practices that resonate well with you, as these are what will carry the highest impact with your results.

Step 1: Identification

The first step to being mindful around stress is identifying the stress. Once you realize you are stressed out, even if you're just slightly stressed, you can start to uncover what is causing that stress. After you recognize the stress, you want to start identifying where it is affecting your life. If it is a large amount of stress, it may be affecting your life in many ways. It could affect the way you sleep, socialize, eat, and take care of yourself. If it is a smaller amount of stress, it may be a little harder to detect where it is affecting your life. Still, stress always affects us in one way or another, so identify all of the ways you are being affected by it.

Realizing you are stressed and identifying the symptoms are the first major key in making sure that you are being mindful around the stress. You have already become mindful of its existence and the impact it has on your life. The next step is to identify where the stress is coming from. Some people recognize the trigger immediately, but others do not. It may be possible for you to think your stress is coming from one area when in reality it is coming from somewhere else. For example, you may think you are stressed out from work, but the real problem is you're not resting enough so you're stressed from being too tired. Once you identify the true culprit of the stress, you can start making changes to eliminate the stress.

Step 2: Eliminating the Stress

This process can be more difficult, especially if the source of your stress is large or carries a heavy emotional value for you. It is extremely important however, as this is the process where all of your results will come from. Later in this book, you will learn about easy and practical applications for mindfulness practices, but for now, you simply need to understand the goal.

The goal in this step is to get into the cause of the stress and eliminate it. Much like picking a weed from a garden, you need to eliminate it from the roots. If you eliminate it only from the base and not the roots, then you are going to find that it will come back in the future, and it may even come back worse. You need to resolve the issue entirely so that it is no longer a problem for you. This can be extremely hard. Once again, if the cause of the stress holds a high emotional value for you, you may struggle to work through it. Some things you can do to make it easier include journaling, getting support, and asking for help. You may not always be able to do it on your own, and having advice and support from others can be extremely helpful.

For some issues, eliminating the stress will take as little as one or two actions. For others, it may take weeks of efforts and practice before you eliminate it. You may even fail a few times at eliminating it before it resolves entirely. The most important thing is that you keep working at it until the issue is no longer present for you. As you start working through it more and more and you start feeling the benefits of the outcome, you will likely find that it is much easier for you to continue working because of that. Soon enough, the issue will be resolved entirely, and you will be able to move on from the ailment.

Step 3: Releasing the Rest

Eliminating the stress can be stressful in itself, and you want to make sure that you release anything that comes up throughout this process. Especially when we have high emotional attachment to certain situations, it can stir up a lot of emotions that need to be worked through. The mindful approach is to recognize these emotions and practice releasing them in a healthy way. Once you do, you will feel definitely better, and you will see that the more you release, the easier everything feels in the long run.

Step 4: Create Healthy New Habits

Once you eliminate a stress and release the emotions around the elimination process, you can identify a new habit you want to implement and start using it. Using the previous example, if you are stressed due to a lack of rest, you may wish to start going to bed earlier or eliminate distractions from the bedroom to make falling asleep easier. Identifying the healthy replacement habits might be easy, or it might be difficult. If the habit seems new and daunting to you, you may wish to start implementing it slowly so that it's easier for you to adopt into your lifestyle. When you are choosing healthy new habits, choose ones that are realistic to you. If you choose new habits that have no emotional value to you, you are likely not going to keep them for long, and you will revert back to old patterns. For example, if you are someone who dislikes running and doesn't have a strong desire to start but you try to implement a new routine to run every evening to help tire you out because you heard it would help, you likely won't keep the habit for long. Instead, you want to pick something that is going to be comfortable for you and make it easy for you to practice in your daily life. The new healthy habit needs to be enjoyable and reasonable so that it lasts, and you do not end up reverting back to unhealthy patterns and recreating stress in your life again. If you find yourself slipping back into old patterns, identify the triggers causing the slip and make necessary changes to keep yourself from regressing.

Step 5: Maintenance

After all is said and done, you will want to maintain your mindfulness practice around stress. Complete the above steps any time you notice stress in your life, no matter how big or small the stress is. If you choose coping methods that do not seem to be working for you, try and discover why and then choose new ones that work better. Part of the mindfulness practice is exploring what works and doesn't work for you and understanding why. When you do this, you learn more about yourself and create the perfect environment for you to continue down your mindfulness journey. Think of this as a working relationship where you will always have to put effort into mindfulness and into learning more about yourself. The more you learn and grow, however, the deeper the connection comes and the easier it is to navigate the journey even during harder times.

Mindfulness has a powerful ability to help eliminate stress and make life a lot easier to manage. It may be difficult to use mindfulness around stress at first, especially if you have a lot of it your life. Start by identifying the largest source of stress and then work your way down from there. With some time, effort, and maintenance, you will find yourself leading a stress-free life thanks to your mindfulness practices. Remember, just because you are being mindful doesn't mean stress won't arise. It simply means that your approach to stress will be altered, and therefore, it will not affect you on the same level that it once did. Instead of infesting your life and ruling it, it will simply be recognized as a trigger to make some changes and start honoring yourself and your needs in a new way.

You are halfway done!

Congratulations on making it to the halfway point of the journey. Many try and give up long before even getting to this point, so you are to be congratulated on this. You have shown that you are serious about getting better every day. I am also serious about improving my life, and helping others get better along the way. To do this I need your feedback. Click on the link below and take a moment to let me know how this book has helped you. If you feel there is something missing or something you would like to see differently, I would love to know about it. I want to ensure that as you and I improve, this book continues to improve as well. Thank you for taking the time to ensure that we are all getting the most from each other.

Chapter 3: Staying in the Moment

Staying in the moment is one of the best ways to enjoy life to its fullest. When you stay in the moment, you experience everything that every moment has to offer. You give yourself the best opportunity to really absorb the joy that comes with life, as well as understand every lesson and experience that is sent your way. Sometimes, especially when the moment is painful or stress is present, staying in the moment can be really difficult. Other times, we are so used to being away from the moment that we struggle to stay in the moment at all. There are many wonderful practices you can use to stay in the moment. Again, which practices you use will greatly depend on what kind of personality you have and what you prefer. In the next chapter, you will learn about practical mindfulness applications.

Using mindfulness as a guide to stay in the moment is a great strategy. The general outline for how you use mindfulness for this purpose is the same for most people, it is merely the practices that change from person to person. When you want to stay mindful of each moment, the following steps will help you with the process.

Step 1: Identify When You Leave the Moment

The first step to staying in the moment is identifying the minute you left the moment. The second you stop being in the moment is exactly what you need to identify. Once you do, you will find it significantly easier for you to make the necessary changes. Identifying the moment can be hard, as it may happen when you aren't paying attention. If you are so used to leaving that it comes naturally to you, you may check about the very fact that you have left. This can make the entire process a lot more difficult. If this is true for you, the simple fact of realizing that you have left helps significantly. For others, you may already be well aware of when or why you have left.

Something to consider is that when a situation is emotionally charged, we often leave because we want to protect ourselves from the situation. We do not want to experience the painful emotions, so we leave as a means to shield ourselves from what we believe is coming next. If you are in a situation where you are leaving because of emotions, there are two things you need to think about. First, these are the situations you need to do work around. These are the ones where you need to identify what is causing you to leave and how you can make changes so that you can stay in the moment. Second, you need to stay because there is a valuable lesson to be learned and you won't learn it by leaving. When you are ready, get back in and experience the lesson.

If you are unaware of when or why you are leaving or there doesn't seem to be a specific cause, then simply realizing that you have left is enough. Realize when you have left, and affirm to yourself that you have done so. Then, move on to step two.

Step 2: Be within Yourself

Before you are back into the situation, you need to be within yourself. If something has caused you to leave, what is it? Why are you leaving? What is making you feel the need to go inwards or mentally remove yourself from the situation? Try and identify as much around the situation as possible. Sometimes, the answer may simply be that you were bored. Other times, there may be a more complex or painful answer. The most important thing is that you take the time to identify the answer. Then, you can figure out what to do about it.

Regardless of why you left, take a minute to recognize what actions you took when you left. Did you start thinking about other things? Did you stop listening to the people around you? Did you pick up your phone and start blankly scrolling news feeds or otherwise showing that you were not present in the moment? Take the time to identify what your patterns and behaviors are when you leave the moment. These are the patterns and behaviors that you are going to want to use to your advantage, as they will become your triggers to help you recognize when you have left in the future.

Step 3: Be Present

By now, you should be aware that you left, maybe have a reason as to why, and have a clear idea of what you do when you leave. Now, you can practice becoming present. If you are completely away, take your time and start bringing yourself back into the moment. You can use any number of the practices described in the next chapter, as long as the outcome is that you feel more present in the moment. The majority of the process will be based on grounding. If there is a negative or uncomfortable emotional value to the situation, you may want to take note of that so you can deal with it now or at a more reasonable time.

As you stay in the moment, let yourself start to experience everything more fully. When distracting thoughts or feelings of getting out come around, simply let them roll off your back and do what you can to stay focused in the moment. It can take time to master this process, but soon enough, you will be able to easily get back in when you have left.

Step 4: Maintenance

As with other mindfulness practices, there is a maintenance that needs to be done to ensure that you stay more frequently. If you are brand new to being in the moment, you will likely struggle to stay for long periods of time. The most important thing is that you do not go hard on yourself. Give yourself space and time to adjust to the new practices and let yourself get used to the idea. Whenever you recognize you're not being present, simply regather your focus and get back in the moment again. The more you become practiced with this, the easier it will be.

Being present in the moment is another working relationship. You will not always be present in the moment, no matter how developed your mindfulness practices are. When you are experiencing high emotions or are having stress in your life, which you will, you will likely leave a lot more frequently. The mindful approach is to recognize when you are leaving and if there is an emotional value to the reason why, such as stress or grief, you do what you can to eliminate the root of the problem and resolve the issues. Then, you can carry on with your mindfulness practice and staying in the moment.

Mindfulness is the best way to stay present in the moment. Being present in the moment is one of the major purposes behind mindfulness practices. When you are present in the moment, whether the moment feels good or not, you gain so much more from it. You learn lessons about yourself, you experience things more deeply, and you open yourself up to a greater opportunity to experience joy. Even the moments that don't feel good are valuable. You learn about how they make you feel, the triggers that you have, and the things that you can do to work through those triggers in a way that feels good for you.

Chapter 4: Easy Application

Mindfulness practices vary based on what you need from your practice, but ultimately, they all have the same goal: to help you achieve a mindful state. These practices are easy to apply in your life, and they are extremely practical. You do not need to set aside several minutes or hours in a day to complete these tasks. In fact, if you do not desire, you don't even need to have a scheduled time in the day where you practice mindfulness. Though, it is recommended. The most important thing is that the techniques you use are ones that feel good to you and help you achieve the primary goal: to become mindful.

Grounding Techniques

When you are feeling particularly overwhelmed with emotions or you find that you are struggling to stay present in the moment, grounding techniques are very powerful. They can help get you out of your head and bring you back into the present and address situations with a more mindful and tactful approach.

5, 4, 3, 2, 1!

Perhaps one of the most popular grounding methods is the 5, 4, 3, 2, 1 method. This method is quite simple and allows you to identify your surroundings quickly and stay more focused on them. You can complete it by first identifying five things that you see, and then four things that you can feel (physically). Then, you can identify three things you hear, two things you smell, and one thing you taste. Take your time as you work through each step and really let yourself experience the process. The point is to absorb more of your surroundings and release your dominant thoughts. Doing so will make it much easier for you to come back into the present moment and stay aware of your real life situation. This is a great technique for any situation where grounding might be needed. You can do it quietly in your head or say it out loud if you feel comfortable doing so in your given situation.

Light Beams

Another great grounding technique is to imagine that you are being pierced by a light beam. The beam should start in the sun and work its way through the top of your head and down your spine. Then, it will come out the bottom of your tail bone and connect into the center of the Earth. When you imagine this light beam, it helps you remember that you are connected to everything and we are one. There is nothing that separates you from the Earth, nor the sun or anything else. If you are feeling an overwhelming amount of emotions, you may wish to imagine the light beam carrying them away and releasing them into the Earth to be eliminated completely.

Firm Roots

Some people prefer to use roots as their grounding technique. Instead of imagining a light beam, they choose to imagine that there are roots under their feet that are firmly connecting them to the ground. These roots are planted in the Earth, and they cannot possibly be separated from it any easier than a massive tree could be. You can imagine yourself developing roots by first taking a deep breathing into your diaphragm and then filling your lungs. As you breathe it out, imagine roots growing from the bottom of your feet and into the Earth beneath you. Feel your feet firmly planted on the ground and recognize that you are connected to the Earth, and there is nothing that can take you away from that.

Triggered Practices

When you are feeling triggered by a particular situation or subject, you will want to use a mindfulness practice to help you through the situation. When you are mindful in triggered situations, you have greater control over yourself. You eliminate reactions and increase your ability to respond in a way that feels comfortable and appropriate for you. This gives you greater control over yourself in the situation, which can allow you to gain virtually anything you want from it. You cannot control the situation you are in, but you can control how it impacts you.

Recognize, Analyze, and Release

Perhaps the best way to respond to a triggered event is to practice the recognize, analyze, and release method. This essentially means that you recognize you have been triggered, analyze everything that comes up with the trigger, and then release it. When you are analyzing the trigger, you will want to see what caused you to feel a certain way, as well as the emotions and feelings that came up when you did feel that way. You should also take the time to analyze anything else that may arise in your personal situation as you are analyzing the situation. Then, once you are aware of everything, release it. If you need to, you can keep track of things that really stood out to you and work on them when you have the time to do releasing methods. If you have the time right away, then of course you should do it. However, if you still have to do things and are not in a space where you can take a few minutes to yourself, simply imagine that, as you breathe out, the issue is exhaled as well and you are released from the feelings, emotions, and thoughts until you are ready to revisit them. It is imperative that you revisit them soon, within 24 hours if possible. This will prevent them from becoming suppressed and turning into a larger problem.

Take Five

When you are triggered by something and you have a bit of time, spending time on the trigger is a good idea. Take a short break if you can, such as by heading outside, to the bathroom, or to another quiet place. When you are there, take a few deep breaths and visualize the experience the moment you were triggered. What did it feel like? What was your initial reaction? Similar to recognize, analyze, and release, ask yourself questions that will help you identify the situation and how it made you feel inside. As you do, take the time to really pay attention to everything. Even take the time to pay attention to your present thoughts and feelings as you continue to analyze the situation. Once you are aware, you can spend the last part of your break doing deep belly breaths. These are a great release mechanism that can help you bring yourself back to the center and feel more at peace as you get back to your day. If you find that there are prominent feelings or stressors that are still present after your break, you should take time to revisit these when you have enough time to sit and focus on them for a while.

Deep Belly Breaths

Deep belly breaths are some of the best ways to relax yourself when you are struggling in the moment. Whether you are caught off guard or are completely unprepared for a situation ahead, breathing deep into your abdomen can help relax you. When we are in difficult or tense situations, we tend to get into a space where we are not breathing deep enough. We may even start breathing extremely shallow ones without even realizing it. If you need a quick activity to help you relax in the face of difficulty or uncertainty, deep belly breaths are a great opportunity. Simply breathe in deeply, hold it for a few seconds, and then exhale everything. This will help you release any tension or stress that you may be harboring inside.

Releasing Techniques

Releasing is one of the hardest but most important things we can do when we are experiencing difficult times. When you are going through a tough situation, it can be easy to absorb a variety of unwanted emotions and feelings without even recognizing it. You may even experience symptoms without having any realization as to what is happening. When you do, you need to release what is building up inside of you. Releasing can help you in many ways. It can help you alleviate difficult symptoms immediately, and it can also help you release unwanted emotions that remain after you have finished doing the difficult conscious work.

Visualization

When you are working on releasing unwanted feelings, energies and thoughts, visualization is one of the best practices you can use. You can use guided visualizations or guide yourself through your own visualization; it is completely up to you. To visualize something, you start by taking deep breaths and relaxing. Then, you can close your eyes and imagine yourself in your mind's eye. Picture what you look like and what the world around you will look like. The best part about visualization is that you can go anywhere you want and be anything you want. Visualize whatever makes you feel happy and positive inside. Then, you can visualize yourself releasing anything you're storing in a way that feels good for you. Some people choose to visualize their thoughts, feelings, or emotions as a cloud drifting away, whereas others choose to visualize it as a black smoke that is exhaled and eventually disappears. You may visualize yourself throwing it away or visualize it simply trickling away like a stream. You can make this visualization as personal to yourself as you desire. If you want to, you can follow a guided visualization, which may help you feel more focused if you are not experienced with visualization practices.

When you are visualizing, you will want to add as many senses as you can to the visualization. Imagine what the sights are, what sounds you might hear, and if there are any smells associated with the vision. If there is anything you feel, or taste, imagine that in your mind too. The more vivid you can make the experience, the better. This will make it truly feel as though you have honestly sent away anything you do not want to hold inside of you and will make the healing process much easier afterward.

Meditation

Meditation is always a powerful method for releasing unwanted thoughts, emotions, and feelings. Meditation is an excellent opportunity to quiet your mind when it is in a state of overwhelm or stress. You can meditate by taking deep breaths and closing your eyes. Stay focused on your breath and your body, and let all of your thoughts pass you by. Do not spend time judging the thoughts you have or obsessing over them; just let them come and then let them go again. When you do, they will pass by you easily. If you find yourself dwelling, obsessing, or judging, simply let go of the thought and judgment and then move on. The more you practice, the easier it will be. Let yourself stay in this state for as long as comfortable, and then gently guide yourself back into the room by opening your eyes and stretching out your body.

Deep Breathing

Deep breathing is an excellent tool for nearly any part of the mindfulness process. You can use it for releasing as well. When you are using deep breathing to release unwanted emotions, thoughts, or energies, imagine that each time you breathe out, you are exhaling everything that is unwanted. Then, every time you inhale, you are inhaling positivity, love, and peace. Spend some time taking these deep breaths and imagine the energies flowing in and out in this order until you are able to feel relaxed and released of any tensions or stresses you may be experiencing. You can use this tool as often as you need to achieve and maintain a peaceful state of mind.

Reframing

Sometimes, the best way to release something is to reframe the way you see it. Reframing is a process whereby you become mindful of the situation and work to see the positive in it. For example, imagine you experienced a red light on your way to work. You could curse and blame it for slowing you down. Alternatively, you could thank that red light for allowing you to take your time and experience the process of driving to work. You could appreciate that red lights, and traffic lights in general, are important tools that provide us with the ability to drive safely on the road without getting into accidents at every intersection. Reframing the way in which you see something is a great way to release tension, stress, frustration, anger, and any other unwanted emotion around it. You can reframe almost every situation simply by choosing to find positive elements of the situation and focusing on those instead of the negative elements.

Daily Practices

Mindfulness is best when you practice it on a regular basis. If you use mindfulness only when you feel triggered to or when you are experiencing heightened emotions, you will likely not get very far with your practice. You will also miss out on many of the amazing benefits and may struggle to develop your practice beyond a few thoughts. Daily mindfulness practices are a great way to increase your skills and see better results from your practices when you truly need mindfulness. You can use these mindfulness practices at least once a day, and they will help you increase the power of your practice immensely. Each practice does not take too long to complete, and you will find that you experience greater peace, freedom, and presence when you do.

Mindful Thinking

Thinking mindfully means that you not only become aware but also aim about the thoughts you have throughout the day. It may seem difficult, especially considering the amount of thoughts we experience on a daily basis. However, once you begin to practice this technique, you will likely find that it is a lot easier than you may think. The first step is to aim to think mindfully and to only have thoughts that serve your greatest good. Set the goal that anything that fails to serve your greatest good will be released effortlessly, and space will be cleared up for more positive thoughts. Once your goal is set, go about your day like you normally would. When you notice what thoughts you are experiencing, either feel happy that you are having positive ones or take action to release negative ones. Then, let yourself feel the joy of knowing that you have intentionally chosen your thoughts. Continue doing so throughout the day whenever you notice to do so. Eventually, you will find that, more often than not, you are completely aware of the thoughts you are having. You will also become aware of the times when your thoughts do not serve you, and you will be able to consciously change them into thoughts that will serve you. You may initially struggle to change your thoughts, and that's okay. The most important thing is that you feel confident and joyful every time you make a positive change. You do not want to punish yourself mentally or in any other way if you are not always successfully able to change your thoughts. Simply do your best and move on. Eventually, it will become extremely easy for you to change them. The most important thing is to practice on a regular basis.

Changing our thoughts can be one of the hardest things we do as humans. Many people feel as though their thoughts are things that are beyond their control and that they simply appear. The truth is, you have full control over your thoughts. You have the ability to shut down any thought you dislike and move on to a more positive thought if you so choose. Knowing that you have that power, you must understand that you also have the ability to increase the number of unwanted and negative thoughts you experience during the day. It is up to you to make the mindful and conscious choice of what thoughts you will support and which ones you won't. Then, take action and change your thoughts to better suit your ideal vision.

Mindful Awareness

Practicing mindful awareness means that you regularly take the time to honestly observe the situation you are in. You take the time to absorb what everything looks, sounds, feels, smells, and tastes like. When you get a gut feeling, you take the time to observe it. If something is particularly bright or patterned in an interesting way, you give yourself the time to observe it. Not only do you observe it, but you also observe the way you feel about it, whether it brings up positive or negative emotions or feelings for you. When you smell something, you take the time to discover whether it is a pleasant smell or a not so pleasant smell for you, and you take the time to explore the feelings it brings up. If you are listening to music, you take the time to listen to the sound and your reaction to the sound. You get the point: any time you are experiencing something and you become aware of the experience, take the time to truly, mindfully observe the experience. Let yourself become aware of what it feels like for you, what it looks like, and how it changes your emotions, if it does at all.

Mindful awareness is a great opportunity to explore your inner self deeper. It also gives you the ability to truly experience the world on a deeper level. When you practice mindful awareness, you stay in the moment and you experience more out of it. You become more skillful at your ability to truly stay in the moment, release stress, and lead a joyful and peaceful lifestyle. You don't have to practice mindful awareness 24/7, but practicing it on a regular basis is important. Whether you choose to practice it at a set time each day or when you feel prompted to by an external experience, the choice is yours.

Mindful Eating

Eating is a wonderful time to become mindful. These days, eating is less about the experience and more about the process of getting as much food down as you can that you don't feel full and then go rushing back to your busy life. This isn't true for everyone, but for many people, it is the case. Even if you don't find yourself rushing your meal, you can likely observe many instances where you do not actually take the time to fully experience your meal either. When you eat mindfully, you take the time to truly absorb the experience. You spend time looking at your food and smelling it, as well as truly tasting it. You chew slowly and swallow when you are done tasting everything in each bite. You take your time between bites and let yourself truly experience the entire moment. When you are full, you simply stop eating. You will likely feel a lot better after meals because you have eaten slowly enough that you can become aware of when you are full and you don't become ill a few moments later when you have eaten too much too quickly.

You can extend this mindful practice to drinking beverages as well. There is no need to gulp back water every now and again to ward off dehydration or when you feel like you can't go another moment without a sip. Instead, become mindful over your drinking habits. Watch as your cup fills with water, and spend time tasting the water as you drink it. Give yourself a chance to think about how the water feels in your mouth when you swallow it. Experience the entire process, and let yourself feel how great it is afterwards when you are done hydrating yourself. Both eating and drinking can be greatly enhanced by mindfulness practices. You prevent yourself from over eating or drinking too quickly and, as a result, increase the value you actually gain from your meals and beverages. You also reduce the chance of you feeling sick afterward.

Mindful Breathing

Breathing arises in every instance of mindfulness because it truly is a powerful practice. In daily mindful breathing, you do not need to become in control over your breath. There is no need to change the tempo, practice deep breathing, or count the breaths. Instead, you simply want to become aware of your own natural and unique breathing pattern. Spend time focusing on your inhalation and exhalation, and how your body feels when you take in and release the air as well. Let yourself fully experience what it is like to breathe and how your body feels when you absorb the oxygen. Imagine what it looks like when the oxygen purifies your cells and cleanses your system. Give yourself a few minutes to really think about your own unique breathing pattern.

If you do notice that your breathing seems shallow or that you are breathing in a way that does not feel comfortable for you, take the time to identify why you think your breathing is like that. Is it simply because you were not paying attention? Or do you feel any emotion that are causing you to have restricted or shallow breaths? If anything comes up, spend some time meditating on it and releasing it. Also, spend time focusing on your breathing pattern and bringing it back to a normal and fulfilling breath.

Mindful Appreciation

Gratitude is a powerful tool you can use to help increase the joy you experience in life. When you are mindful about appreciation and gratitude, you spend time purposefully acknowledging the things you have in life and showing appreciation for them. You acknowledge things no matter what size they are, and you spend time making sure that you show appreciation for them. You might show appreciation for your home, your car, the gas you fuel your car with, or even a pen that you use to fill out your daily journaling. You might want to show appreciation for family and friends, strangers who do kind things such as holding the door open, or stop lights that help guide traffic and keep everyone safe on the road. Mindful appreciation helps you realize the importance of everything in your environment and truly feel grateful for each item. When you show gratefulness and appreciation in this way, you become more joyful and attract more joy into your life. You aim to think positive thoughts that serve your greatest good, and you also aim to serve the greatest good of the collective.

Mindful Listening

Listening is sometimes an activity we take for granted. We listen to others only to formulate our own answers and opinions on what they are saying. We don't always hear exactly what they say because we are too busy hearing what we want to hear. This isn't always the case, but in many situations, it is. Very few people have strong, active, and mindful listening skills making them powerful listeners. When you listen mindfully, you listen with the aim to hear what you are being told. You do not formulate judgments or opinions until all of the information has been received, and even when in some instances, you do not formulate them at all. You spend time truly watching the person who is talking and understanding what they are saying to you. When you listen mindfully, you are aware of the emotions of the person who is speaking and the nonverbal communication they are sharing with you through their language. You hear the entire message, instead of snippets that stuck out to you.

When people take the time to mindfully listen, information is shared a lot easier. Relationships form deeper connections, arguments are avoided, and people feel heard and appreciated. Listening mindfully allows you the opportunity to truly understand the people you are communicating with and allows them the opportunity to truly feel understood. It is a great chance for you to absorb as much as possible from conversations you have and prevent possible miscommunications due to a lack of effective listening skills. This is a skill we often take for granted, but it is important that we learn to master it.

Body Scans

Daily body scans are a powerful way to tune into your body and feel into your emotions. These scans are mental examinations you do to your entire body: physical, emotional, and energy-wise. You take time to acknowledge how you are actually feeling. When we are busy in our daily lives, we tend to ignore our body and fail to listen to what it is telling us until it is quite literally screaming. We miss symptoms of illnesses until they become full-blown diseases, we miss symptoms of stress until we are no longer able to handle the pressure, and we miss many other things until we reach a point where we can no longer ignore them.

Think about a salt water tank. Each piece of life in the tank is vital to the survival of the entire tank. The fish, coral, and plants are all important, as well as the salt water and the sand. If any of the elements were missing or damaged, the entire tank would die. Hobbyists spend a small amount of time each day monitoring everything in the tank to ensure it is maintained properly. They adjust water temperatures and mineral levels, observe the living elements to make sure they are interacting well, and make any necessary changes to optimize the health of the entire tank. If the tank were left for even just a week, the levels could change drastically, and the entire tank would begin to spiral out of control. The water quality would dwindle, and the living elements of the tank would die off as well. Of course, if someone noticed the levels were off, they would likely be able to save it, but it would take drastic measures to do so. However, if they spent a little time each day maintaining the tank, they could avert any of these situations by recognizing them in advance and taking appropriate actions immediately.

Your body works in much the same way. Your physical body, emotions, feelings, energies, and everything else are all tied together. If one begins to suffer, the rest begin to suffer as well. Your body, emotions, feelings and energies will quickly spiral out of control until you reach a state where you either make a change or fade away to illness or otherwise. Of course, it takes us much longer than a week to completely spiral that far, and in many times, our bodies will give us major symptoms to indicate that we need to pay attention. However, the more we ignore, the worse the situation becomes.

A body scan works by taking a moment to relax and sit or lie down comfortably. Then, you start slowly considering how you feel in each part of your body, from the top of your head to the bottom of your feet. As you do, take note of any areas that may not feel good for you. Let yourself understand what these feelings are and where they come from. If you are feeling grief, for example, you may feel it in your chest area. If you are feeling dehydrated, you may feel it in your throat and head area. Any symptoms or feelings you are having will be felt somewhere in your body. When you do feel them, identify exactly where they are resting and spend time mindfully working through them and then releasing them. Give love to yourself and to any feelings you are having. Take the time to work through them. Manage your system before it is completely filled with toxicity and you are forced to tune in, in one way or another.

Many people believe that mindfulness is a highly spiritual practice, and for many people, it is. For others, however, it is a logical practice that is used to improve the quality of life and increase one's ability to cope with difficult situations. Regardless of how you choose to see the practices, they are highly beneficial and can add value to anyone's life. When you practice mindfulness on a regular basis, specifically on a daily basis, you increase the value you gain from your practice. You improve your life overall as your mental health and physical health increase. When you take the time to tune in and truly work through any issues you may be experiencing inside, you give yourself the opportunity to heal yourself and move on in life. You prevent yourself from becoming weighted down by difficult emotions or physical symptoms, and you move yourself into a space where you can heal and move on lightly. Mindfulness is a powerful practice to eliminate stress, promote peace and happiness, and teach people to live in the moment.

Chapter 5: Mindfulness Mastery

If you are someone who takes what you do seriously, you will likely want to know how you can go from "beginner" to "master". Of course, this book is a complete guide, and the goal is to teach you how you can become a mindfulness master. These techniques, tips, and guidelines are designed to help you understand how you can enhance your practice and increase the value you gain from it. These techniques are not necessarily all mindfulness practices on their own, but they are practices that will significantly enhance the quality of your own practice and, therefore, the results you gain from it.

Tips to Enhance Mindfulness Practice

When you are in the process of practicing mindfulness techniques, there are things that you can do to increase the value you gain from your practice. You can use these tips to make sure that your practice is successful and you get the most out of it that you possibly can. These tips are great for beginners who are looking to master the practice.

Slow Down

Some people want to practice mindfulness and master it all in the same day. While you can master mindfulness easily, the trick is not to rush yourself. The slower you go, the faster you'll master this practice. Using the techniques you have learnt in this book, take the time to teach yourself how to successfully do each one. When you find the ones that resonate with you, make these your "signature moves" and practice them frequently. Get to know them and how they serve you. Learn to understand what it feels like for you when you do this, and pay attention for opportunities to increase the quality of your results. Make it intimate and personal, and watch as your results explode. Slow down and take some of the pressure off of yourself. The process of mindfulness is largely related to the process of getting to know yourself, and as with any relationship, it takes time to truly become amazing at it. Give yourself the time to get there.

Focus on Concentration

A skill you should emphasize when you are learning about mindfulness and are wanting to master it is concentration. You should spend an enormous amount of time focusing on concentration when you are starting out, and you should seek to maintain your skill of concentration as you carry on. Concentration is a powerful tool that will help you stay focused on what you are trying to do and will prevent you from losing yourself to distractions. At first, distractions are rampant, and it is inevitable that you will become distracted in the process. To develop concentration, you can practice this skill all on its own. To do so, gather an object that you find intriguing to look at and place it in front of you. Look at the object and do your best to recognize all of the physical elements of the object. Observe the texture, color, shape, and size. Also observe your emotional and physical reactions to the object. Whenever you find yourself getting distracted, focus on the object again. Over time, you will find it much easier to focus on the object and stay focused for a long period of time. This focus and concentration will help you master everything using your mindfulness practice.

Start Simple

Relationships start with "hello" or something simple. The best relationships start with a small but sturdy foundation and gradually develop as one learn more about the other person, and everything grows from there. The same goes for mindfulness. Start with simple practices. Perhaps all you want to start with is recognizing when things trigger you and taking the time to become aware of your emotional and physical response to the trigger. Eventually, once you become practiced at recognizing the triggers, you will be able to implement a change to improve how you respond to the situation. When beginning, however, just stay focused on starting simple. The more you practice and successfully use mindfulness to change your life for the better, the easier it will be to use these techniques on larger and more emotionally charged situations.

Be Gentle on Yourself

Mindfulness should be a positive strategy that you use to eliminate stress and stay present in the moment. Being harsh on yourself when you do not succeed to your desired standards will do the exact opposite; it will get you stuck in your head and cause you to stress out. Instead, be gentle and kind to yourself. If you recognize a trigger several moments, hours, or even days after it occurred, don't become angry with yourself for not recognizing it in the moment. Instead, celebrate yourself for recognizing it at all. The same goes for any goal you have with mindfulness. Maintain the positive associations with the practice by being gentle to yourself and celebrating all of your wins. Use "losses" as a milestone: events that occurred, which taught you a lesson about yourself and your life. Then, absorb the information from the lesson, so you can use it in the future. We all take time to get from point A to point B, and you are no different. Be kind to yourself and your practice will flourish in no time.

Be Patient with Yourself

For the same reason why you want to be gentle to yourself, you should be patient too. If it takes you several weeks to successfully complete goals you have set out for yourself, don't get stressed because it is taking you longer than you desired. It is likely that you are learning a great deal about yourself along the way and that you are gaining more than you could have possibly imagined when you embarked on the journey. Give yourself time, and let yourself embrace each experience. A large part of being mindful is being able to recognize that you are not always in control of the situation, and sometimes, you will benefit from letting go completely and simply going with the flow of things. Again, the slower you go, the faster your practice will develop. Be easy on yourself, and refrain from setting any timelines with your goals. As long as you are making steady progress, consider that a success and keep doing what you are doing. If you notice areas where you may be able to improve your practice to increase your success, of course, do so. But do not feel that a slower pace is the result of failure. It is absolutely not true. Be patient with yourself.

Learn to Let Go

Many people struggle to let go of things, and a big part of being mindful is learning to let go. There are many instances where you will be triggered, but there will be absolutely nothing you can do. The mindful approach to these situations is to learn to let go. Use the releasing techniques taught in this book, and release the emotions or feelings you have generated around the experience. You are not required to hold on to everything that you experience in life. Whether you had emotional or mental work to do around the situation or not, when all is said and done, learn to effectively let go. At first, you might struggle with this as we tend to hold on to the things that affect us. This is because on a biological level, the things that hurt us are a "threat", and we must avoid them to be able to survive. The reality is that we are far more advanced than that, and the majority of our perceived threats really are not threats at all. A good idea is to have a set period of time each day where you let go of the day. Anything that has upset you, stressed you out, or otherwise taken up space in your mind can be released, and you can allow yourself to thoroughly relax and rest for the night. When you do this, you will find that you sleep better, and your stress levels are much lower overall.

Make It Fun

You wouldn't stay friends with someone who was too serious or boring, would you? Mindfulness does not have to be a serious or boring experience. In fact, there are many ways that you can incorporate mindfulness into your life and make it a thrilling experience. One of the best practices for mindfulness is learning to stay in the present moment. When you stay present in the moment, you experience the moment much greater. Use your practice in moments that present a great amount of joy and happiness, and you will absorb an unbelievable amount of that. There is no reason for the practice to be all boring and serious all of the time. While you are going to want to stay present in difficult moments and work through those as well, it doesn't have to be all about that.

Adjust It to Suit Your Needs

Everyone is different in many ways. There are no two people who are exactly the same. As a result, you should recognize that your mindfulness practice will not be the same as others either. You will find that some techniques work better than others for you, and over time, you will develop your own unique concoction of techniques and strategies that will fulfill your needs. Take your time and feel free to adjust as necessary. Believe it or not, you will likely be adjusting your strategies and tactics for your entire life when you are practicing mindfulness. As we grow and evolve, our needs do as well. As a result, so does our mindfulness practice.

Tips for Staying Committed

Some people struggle to stay committed to new habits. The reality is that mindfulness is a complete lifestyle change. You cannot achieve mindfulness and then have it forever; instead, you must work to keep the balance of mindfulness in your life on a regular basis. The following tips are great for helping people stay committed to their practice.

Practice for at Least 21 Days

They say it takes 21 days for something to officially become a new habit. That being said, if you take the time to practice mindfulness for at least 21 days, it will become a new habit in your life. If you can commit yourself to three weeks of practicing mindfulness on a daily basis, you will find that by the end of the three weeks it comes as a second nature to you. Then, it will be much easier to remember to do it on a regular basis.

Set a Reminder in Your Phone

For some people, an easy way to remember is to set a reminder in your phone. Choose the time of day that best suits your needs, and set the reminder. Then, when your reminder goes off, take a few minutes to practice mindfulness. If you are someone who tends to be busy or if you want to learn to practice mindfulness in your active life and not just when you have the time to have a break, you might want to consider setting several reminders. Have one for the morning, afternoon, and night. Then, whenever the reminder goes off on your phone, you will remember to be mindful over the present situation. This is a great way to ensure that you remember to practice mindfulness.

Have Anchors or Triggers

Some people are not so fond of phone reminders or may not feel that it is enough to help them practice it frequently. If this is the case, you can consciously aim that certain situations, objects, or other anchors will trigger you to practice mindfulness. For example, maybe you aim that every time you see an analog clock you will become mindful over the situation. At first, you may forget about this, but later on, you will find that every time you see an analog clock, you start practicing a mindfulness technique and become more present in the moment. You can set as many or as few anchors as you would like, and they can be anywhere and made from anything. You might choose a piece of jewelry, a certain object you see on a regular basis, or even a specific person to be your anchor. It is completely up to you.

Journal Your Progress

Another great tool for encouraging you to stay committed is a journal. Journals are excellent for helping you track and record your progress throughout the experience. For some people, being able to write down their experiences throughout the day is a great opportunity to remember to practice mindfulness. Whenever you see the journal, you will remember to become mindful, and then, you will be able to track your experience. Then, you have a trigger as well as written proof of just how far you have come.

There are many ways that you can improve your mindfulness practice to help you grow from being a beginner to being a master. The key is to take it slow, get to know your own unique practice, and do whatever you need to in order to stay consistent and committed to the practice. Once you do it long enough, you will start to learn more about yourself and your own unique practice, and soon enough, it will become easier for you to master.

Conclusion

Mindfulness is a powerful practice that can completely transform your life. When you use the tools of mindfulness, you give yourself the opportunity to reduce the amount of stress you experience and teach yourself to become more present in the moment. As a result, you will find that you are more peaceful, positive, joyful, and optimistic in life. You may not be able to completely relieve yourself of all stressors, but you will be able to totally change the way you respond to stressors, which will have a huge impact on your health and well-being.

I hope *Mindfulness for Beginners: Secrets to Getting Rid of Stress and Staying in the Moment* was successful at helping you learn how you can eliminate your stress and stay present in the moment. This book was designed to empower people to feel more confident in not only starting up their own mindfulness practice but also mastering it. Remember, the slower you go and the more you practice and stay committed, the sooner you will become a master and the greater results you will see from your practice.

The next step is to start from the beginning. Take your time and start developing your mindfulness practice by developing your concentration skills and learning to become self-aware of moments as they happen. As you feel more and more comfortable with your practice, you will be able to advance to greater steps and start making real and noticeable changes in your life. Then, your life will transform in front of your very eyes, and you will see how easy it is to control yourself and your reality.

Lastly, if you enjoyed this book, I hope that you will take the time to honestly rate it on Amazon Kindle. Your honest feedback would be greatly appreciated.

Thank you, and good luck.

Help me improve this book

While I have never met you, if you made it through this book I know that you are the kind of person that is wanting to get better and is willing to take on tough feedback to get to that point. You and I are cut from the same cloth in that respect. I am always looking to get better and I wish to not just improve myself, but also this book. If you have positive feedback, please take the time to leave a review. It will help other find this book and it can help change a life in the same way that it changed yours. If you have constructive feedback, please also leave a review. It will help me better understand what you, the reader, need to make significant improvements in your life. I will take your feedback and use it to improve this book so that it can become more powerful and beneficial to all those who encounter it.

Free membership into the Mastermind Self Development Group!

For a limited time, you can join the Mastermind Self Development Group for free! You will receive videos and articles from top authorities in self development as well as a special group only offers on new books and training programs. There will also be a monthly member only draw that gives you a chance to win any book from your Kindle wish list!

If you sign up through this link http://www.mastermindselfdevelopment.com/specialreport you will also get a special free report on the Wheel of Life. This report will give you a visual look at your current life and then take you through a series of exercises that will help you plan what your perfect life looks like. The workbook does not end there; we then take you through a process to help you plan how to achieve that perfect life. The process is very powerful and has the potential to change your life forever. Join the group now and start to change your life!
http://www.mastermindselfdevelopment.com/specialreport

You will also love these other great titles from Mastermind Self Development!

You will want to check out these other great titles Mastermind Self Development. All available in the Kindle store or you can just click on covers below.

getBook.at/mindfulnessforbeginners

http://mybook.to/positive

You can also find these titles by searching them in the Kindle store on Amazon.

Positive Thinking

30 Days Of Motivation And Affirmations: Change Your "Mindset" & Fill Your Life With Happiness, Success, & Optimism!

By: Robert Norman

© Copyright 2016 - All rights reserved.

In no way is it legal to reproduce, duplicate, or transmit any part of this document in either electronic means or in printed format. Recording of this publication is strictly prohibited and any storage of this document is not allowed unless with written permission from the publisher. All rights reserved.

The information provided herein is stated to be truthful and consistent, in that any liability, in terms of inattention or otherwise, by any usage or abuse of any policies, processes, or directions contained within is the solitary and utter responsibility of the recipient reader. Under no circumstances will any legal responsibility or blame be held against the publisher for any reparation, damages, or monetary loss due to the information herein, either directly or indirectly.

Respective authors own all copyrights not held by the publisher.

Legal Notice:

This book is copyright protected. This is only for personal use. You cannot amend, distribute, sell, use, quote or paraphrase any part or the content within this book without the consent of the author or copyright owner. Legal action will be pursued if this is breached.

Disclaimer Notice:

Please note the information contained within this document is for educational and entertainment purposes only. Every attempt has been made to provide accurate, up to date and reliable complete information. No warranties of any kind are expressed or implied. Readers acknowledge that the author is not engaging in the rendering of legal, financial, medical or professional advice.

By reading this document, the reader agrees that under no circumstances are we responsible for any losses, direct or indirect, which are incurred as a result of the use of information contained within this document, including, but not limited to, —errors, omissions, or inaccuracies.

Free Special Report

Are you interested in taking your life to the next level? Than Mastermind Self Development has an amazing offer for you. For a limited time, we are offering a FREE special report on the Wheel of Life. This report will give you a visual look at your current life and then take you through a series of exercises that will help you plan out what your perfect life looks like. The workbook does not end there; we then take you through a process to help you plan out how to achieve that perfect life. The process is very powerful and has the potential to change your life forever. Take advantage of it now by going to our website! www.mastermindselfdevelopment.com/specialreport

Table of Contents

Summary

Chapter 1: Affirmations – Why They Work and How to Use Them Effectively

Chapter 2: Phase One – Days One Through Eight

Chapter 3: Phase Two – Days Nine Through Fourteen

Chapter 4: Phase Three – Days Fifteen Through Twenty-Two

Chapter 5: Phase Four – Days Twenty-Three Through Thirty

Chapter 6: What if it Doesn't Work?

Chapter 7: Positive Affirmations for Success

Chapter 8: Positive Affirmations for Good Health

Chapter 9: Positive Affirmations for your Career

Chapter 10: Positive Affirmations for Motivation

Chapter 11: Preparing and Using Your Own Affirmations

Conclusion

Summary

Thank you for purchasing my book "Positive Thinking: 30 Days Of Motivation and Affirmations: Change Your "Mindset" & Fill Your Life With Happiness, Success, & Optimism." Choosing this book is the first step to bringing positive thinking into your life, the next step is to follow the day by day instructions as they are listed in the book and watch your life transform before your eyes.

One of the most efficient ways you can improve your life is by simply thinking in a more positive way. This isn't anything new, and probably isn't something that you haven't heard before as it is one of the most common pieces of advice that is given. However, it isn't as easy as it sounds. In fact, it is one of the most difficult things you are going to do. If it were as easy as it sounds, we would be living in a world full of people who see the glass as being half full and people wouldn't struggle with mental health.

You are probably wondering, if being more positive is the most effective way to bring more happiness into our lives, why aren't more of us more positive? There are a few reasons why it is incredibly difficult to become more positive.

How We Think It Is, Is How It Is – It's easy to confuse what has happened in our past as what is going to happen in the future. What we fail to realize is that what happened in our past does not have to equal the future. If you believe that it does, then it does. But, if you believe it doesn't, then it doesn't. It's that simple.

Changing Our Mind Set Is Hard – to become more positive, it is going to require that you change the way you are currently thinking. Changing how you view things isn't easy. Throughout our lives, we are told that things are the way they are. At no point are we told that we have the power to change it. Today I am telling you; you have the authority to change your mindset and become more positive.

Lack Of Energy And Motivation – Changing the way we think isn't easy. It takes a lot of emotional energy. If you are stressed out by work and your personal life and aren't eating or sleeping well you aren't going to have the energy that is required to change how you think. This is especially true if you aren't sure how being more positive is going to benefit you on a personal level.

So how do you get that motivation? How do you learn what the benefits to becoming more positive are? That is where this book comes in. This book is going to provide you with thirty days of affirmations and quotes that are designed to bring more positivity into your life.

This book is going to have each day on its own page, so you aren't distracted by the next day's reading. The thirty days are separated into four "phases" and each phase is going to include a challenge for you to complete throughout that phase. None of these challenges are going to be very difficult, and they were all designed with the purpose of making you more mindful of your thoughts and how they affect you and your life. Each day is going to include a quote as well as an affirmation for you to say to yourself.

What Power Does A Quote Have?

You are probably wondering if reading a quote is going to be enough to change how you are thinking and turn you into a more positive person. The answer is a resounding yes. Quotes have the power to coach us when we can relate to the situation the quote is discussing. They are often inspirational and give us the faith we need to know we are capable of accomplishing something. With each quote that you are going to read in this book, you are going to take the time to think about how it relates to a situation in your life.

What Is An Affirmation?

An affirmation is something you are going to say to yourself to undo the negative self-talk that you are currently experiencing. You might think you aren't experiencing any negative self-talk, but chances are that on some level, you probably are. Negative self-talk covers everything from believing you aren't going to be able to accomplish something to not liking something about yourself.

You are going to say your affirmations to yourself at least twice a day for five minutes at a time. This means that you are going to repeat your affirmation over and over again for that five minutes. Say your affirmation slowly and allow the words to sink into your mind and become a part of your everyday thinking.

By reading these quotes and affirmations on a daily basis, you are reminding yourself every day of all of the good in your life. Quotes and affirmations have the power to change our thinking and help us to see something in ourselves that we want to change or overcome.

How Are Daily Affirmations Going To Help?

There are some great benefits to getting daily inspiration as well as saying daily affirmations.

- You are going to be aware of your daily thoughts and words, which is going to reduce the amount of negative thoughts that are going to be able to enter into your mind.

- The daily practice is going to help you to keep things in life in perspective. In the fast paced life that we currently live in, it is easy to take the good things in life for granted, and even easier to focus on the bad things. Something as simple as an affirmation saying "I am healthy" in the morning is enough to remind you to be grateful for the good things in your life.

- Daily affirmations are great for increasing how positive you are. When you are more positive, you are going to notice more of the great things that are happening in your life and also welcome more blessings and gifts into your life.

- As you become more positive and happy, other people are going to notice. You are going to find yourself helping others without even trying and seeing that is going to help you to stay even more focused.

Don't get discouraged if you struggle to eliminate the negative thoughts completely from your mind immediately. Simply try to change the negative thought into a positive one. If you can't, just let the negative thought go and think about something else instead.

Are you ready to get started? Remember to start on day one and do one page a day until you reach the end. In thirty days you are going to have undergone a complete mental transformation from negative and unhappy to being a positive, happy person on their way to success. Best of luck, enjoy the journey.

Chapter 1: Affirmations – Why They Work and How to Use Them Effectively

"Affirmations are our mental vitamins, providing the supplementary positive thoughts we need to balance the barrage of negative events and thoughts we experience daily." – Tia Walker

It would be so easy for us to toss positive affirmations aside as nothing more than new-age nonsense, a habit that is practiced only by those who are gullible. But there are too many success stories for this and, provided you use them in the right way, you will find that positive affirmations are incredibly powerful, a true aid to success and happiness throughout your life.

Unless you don't have the Internet or the television, you cannot have missed the strong and ever-growing popularity of positive affirmations. They are just about everywhere you look, even on pictures, cups and table coasters. But what are they exactly and why do they work?

What is an Affirmation?

An affirmation is the practice of thinking positively and of empowering yourself. They normally take the form, as you will see throughout this book, of short statements that you must repeat to yourself to create reality in your life. These affirmations are always in the present tense, never past and definitely never future.

While cynical people may choose to write these off as having no meaning, as thoughts that we simply repeat to ourselves instead getting down to the work of actually making plans for action, affirmations actually play a very big part in the work that you do to mold the career that you want and, provided they are used in the right way, they can help you to get to your destination, taking the right route and with confidence. And, rather than being something we invented just recently, affirmations have actually been about for a very long time, conceived originally by a man in the medical profession

A Short History of Affirmations

The man who is considered to be responsible for affirmations is a French pharmacist and psychologist by the name of Emile Coue. Back in the early twentieth century, he noticed that, when he gave patients a potion and told them, at the same time, just how effective it was, he got better results than with those he said nothing to.

It was then that he realized our minds are constantly occupied by thoughts and that these thoughts became reality, a kind of autosuggestion when he told his patients to repeat these words every day – *"Every day, in every way, I am getting better and better"*. Throughout his work, Coue was responsible for achieving a large number of cures, many of them remarkable, but he also failed in a way as well. He came to the conclusion that, if his patients could make an independent judgment about the affirmations they were saying, his methods would not work and his conclusion was that, for an affirmation to work, you have to truly believe it.

Why Not All Affirmations Work

That belief is one of the stumbling points of affirmations. Yes, you can say to yourself over and over again, "my post-baby career is amazing" but, unless you actually believe that, deep inside of you and with all of your heart, it simply won't work.

You can choose a mantra and you can repeat it every single day but there is no way you can fool the very core of you and if you want your mantra to come true, you have to have the deepest of true beliefs in it. Sadly, this is why many people fail with affirmations and I will talk more about this in a later chapter but, we tend to believe that our mantras have to be ambitious otherwise there is no point. Dream a big dream or don't dream at all and that is not the way affirmations work.

We also make the mistake of looking for affirmations that someone else has come up with, that we can use for our own purposes without really making sure that they work for us. To show you how some affirmations are badly or poorly written, take a look at these:

- Saying to yourself, *"I am as thin as a supermodel and well-toned"* isn't going to work when what you see in the mirror is the baby weight you are struggling to shed and you haven't been anywhere near a gym in, well, forever.
- Saying to yourself, *"I am running the most successful multinational company"* won't work if your main way of filling your time through the week is sat down watching television.
- Saying to yourself, *"I am wealthy beyond everything I dreamed of"* definitely won't work if you can't find the money to pay your bills and haven't treated yourself to any new clothes or shoes in months

There is a danger in picking an affirmation that doesn't fit with how you actually feel and that is that it can make you do the complete opposite of what you wanted. Instead of a feeling of empowerment and positivity, you end up throwing the towel in, thinking to yourself that where you actually want to be is so far away from where you actually are, and you'll never be able to get there so there really isn't any point in trying.

What do you do? Forget your affirmations, throw them all away and go back to how you were. That is absolutely the wrong thing to do. What you have to do is pick the right affirmations, or write your own, and use them in the right way.

Finding the Right Affirmation

So, how do you pick the affirmation that is going to work for you? In a lot of ways, it is similar to a SMART goal:

- **S**pecific
- **M**easured
- **A**chievable
- **R**ealistic
- **T**ime-Related

First, your affirmation must not be vague. Saying something like, "*I have a fantastic career*" isn't really giving your subconscious anything to work with and it is too broad to generate any true conviction. It will also not help you to realize when you have achieved your goal. Instead, you should consider something that is near enough to your situation at the current time to be achievable and realistic. Then find or write an affirmation around it. A couple of examples would be:

- I enjoy what I do and I am truly appreciated for it
- I am on a journey that will help me run my own company
- I respond calmly to stressful situations
- I am confident and completely at ease in my job interview

These may be slightly above what you are actually feeling right now because they are describing something that you desire, not something that you cannot attain. They will also let you take the right action for you to achieve them and once you have done that, you move on and come up with a new affirmation for the next big step. Simply match your mantra to your progress, similar to taking a large project and breaking it down into smaller, more manageable projects.

If your affirmation is not achievable, is too ambitious, your core is not going to believe that you can achieve it and that means it will fail.

Create Your Own Personal Affirmations

So, what do you do? Affirmations do work if you use them properly and that means forgetting the one-size-fits-all approach. Yes, you can look for ideas for positive affirmations and, if you find one that fits your situation properly, use it. If not, adapt one or write your own. Tweak existing ones if you need to but make sure they genuinely work for you.

Chapter 2: Phase One – Days One Through Eight

"We first must think 'I can,' then behave appropriately along that line of thought." – Marsha Sinetar

Since this is your first phase, we are going to make your challenge an easy one. This challenge is something you need to accomplish every day, and not just for this week, but on throughout the entire thirty days.

This phase's challenge has been designed to help you be successful at becoming more positive. Making extra time in your day for new goals can be difficult to do. To help offset that, your challenge this week is going to be to get up a few minutes earlier.

Challenge – Phase One: Set your alarm fifteen minutes earlier than what you are getting up at right now. Use those fifteen minutes every morning to read through that day's affirmation and quote. Take your time reading the affirmation and quote and make sure that you read them more than once.

After you have read the quote a couple of times, close your eyes and think about what the quote means to you. Consider how the quote makes you feel and how you can relate to the quote. If how the quote makes you feel is negative, take a note of that and see if you can find a more positive way to frame your feelings.

Each day is also going to have some things that you can take into consideration to help you get started with the thinking process. As you consider each quote and affirmation, feel free to make notes and jot down any thoughts that you connect to them.

Write the affirmation down somewhere that you are going to see it throughout the day. Whether that means that you are going to email it to yourself, write it on a sticky note and place it on your computer or put it on your phone, make sure it is accessible and visible.

Keep three or four of the affirmations in this book together where you can recite them twice a day. You aren't going to want to have more than three or four to recite a day as this is going to create additional mental stress. Choose the ones that you feel apply the most to your life as the ones that you are going to recite to yourself. You can change which ones you are reciting each day as you wish to.

Day One

Quote*:* "You can achieve anything you want in life as long as you have the courage to dream it, the intelligence to make a realistic plan, and the will to see that plan through to the end." – Sidney A. Friedman

Affirmation*:* The power is within me. I learn from the past, live in the now and plan for the future.

Some Things You Should Consider:

While you are thinking about this quote and repeating this affirmation, think about the things in your life that you want to accomplish. Dreams that you haven't pursued because you feel like you won't accomplish them. Think about the challenges you have overcome in the past.

Say this affirmation like you mean it and believe it. Before you go to bed tonight, stand in front of the mirror and look yourself in the eyes. Repeat today's affirmation and tell yourself you are going to be a better person after these thirty days. Continue telling yourself that you are going to be a better person at the end of this thirty days.

Day Two

Quote: "Man often becomes what he believes himself to be. If I keep on saying to myself that I cannot do a certain thing, it is possible that I may end by really becoming incapable of doing it. On the contrary, if I have the belief that I can do it, I shall surely acquire the capacity to do it even if I may not have it at the beginning." — Mahatma Gandhi

Affirmation: I choose to find hopeful and optimistic ways to look at this.

Some Things You Should Consider:

When you are thinking about this quote, consider what you believe yourself to be. If you find yourself using negative words to describe yourself, try to replace as many as those negative ideas with a positive twist on them.

Anytime you are faced with a struggle, repeat the affirmation above. Whether this is a personal struggle, a work struggle, or a financial struggle, this affirmation is going to help you through it. After you have repeated this affirmation when you are struggling for a while, you are going to find yourself naturally looking for a more optimistic approach to a situation without having to give it any thought.

Day Three

Quote: "Once Your Mindset changes, everything on the outside will change along with it." – Steve Maraboli

Affirmation: I clearly see the beauty of life that flourishes around me

Some Things You Should Consider:

While you are thinking about this quote, consider how you look at things. Consider whether you are the kind of person who sees beauty in things or notices the ugliness around them. If you are the kind of person who sees the ugliness, think about how you can see the beauty around you instead.

While you go about your day today, consider all of the amazing things that are around you. From the flower growing in the garden to the bird flying overhead, there is beauty in all things, when you can see the beauty in these things you are going to be able to accomplish more.

Day Four

Quote*:* "The true secret of happiness lies in taking a genuine interest in all the details of daily life." – William Morris

Affirmation*:* For me, happiness is a journey, not a destination. I have been blessed with happiness, and my journey is endless.

Some Things You Should Consider:

Consider the parts of your day that bring you the most happiness. What is it about those parts of your day that make you happy? Think about the things that are all around you during those parts of the day. Consider the people, the noise levels, the smells, tastes and anything else that seems important. Take note of all of those details and commit them to your memory.

Day Five

Quote: "Happiness lies in the joy of achievement and the thrill of creative effort" – Franklin D. Roosevelt

Affirmation: Happiness is a choice. I base my happiness on my accomplishments and the blessings I've been given.

Some Things You Should Consider:

Consider the things you have done in your life that make you happy. Think about the people in your life, and the goals you have accomplished that bring your happiness. Realize that even when you weren't successful, the excitement of trying brought you happiness as well.

Anytime you find yourself feeling unhappy with the hand life has dealt you, repeat the affirmation above and remember, happiness is a choice.

Day Six

Quote: "Progress is impossible without change and those who cannot change their minds cannot change anything" – George Bernard Shaw

Affirmation: I have been given endless talents which I begin to utilize today.

Some Things You Should Consider:

If you want to progress towards a happier life, you are going to have to change how you are thinking about things. This isn't as hard as it seems. While you are thinking about this quote, consider opinions or habits you have that you are unwilling to change.

Anytime you find yourself in a situation that cannot be solved in the usual way, think about the affirmation above and remember that you are capable of change, if you just utilize your talents and find a new solution.

Day Seven

Quote: "Don't rely on someone else for your happiness and self-worth. Only you can be responsible for that. If you can't love and respect yourself – no one else will be able to make that happen. Accept who you are – completely; the good and the bad – and make changes as YOU see fit – not because you think someone else wants you to be different."
– Stacey Charter

Affirmation: I love and respect myself as I am.

Some Things You Should Consider:

While you are thinking about the quote above, consider how much you rely on other people to validate you. Are you confident in who you are, or do you need other people to give you positive affirmations to feel like you are worthwhile?

Say this affirmation to yourself as often as you can, until you truly believe it. You cannot become more positive, happier or successful if you don't first love, respect and accept yourself for who you are.

Day Eight

Quote: "Work hard for what you want because it won't come to you without a fight. You have to be strong and courageous and know that you can do anything you put your mind to. If somebody puts you down or criticizes you, just keep on believing in yourself and turn it into something positive." – Leah LaBelle

Affirmation: Giving up is easy, and always an option so I will delay it for another day.

Some Things You Should Consider:

You have made it to the end of the first phase. Congratulations for making it this far. Consider how your thoughts have changed in the last week. Are you beginning to see things in a more positive way? Are you finding that you are happier and feeling more fulfilled?

Anytime you find yourself struggling to motivate yourself to do something, say the affirmation above out loud. Remember, real strength shows itself when you don't quit, and you see something through to the ending.

Success Story – Thomas

"There is nothing in the world that I cannot achieve when I have the courage to believe."

– Chiara Gizzi

My name is Thomas, I am not quite 50 yet and I have been using positive affirmations for more than 20 years, almost constantly. Sometimes they have actually taken my life over and have delved into my pursuits in the biggest ways possible but to me, this is a good thing. Affirmations have given me the opportunity to transform myself in the most positive ways and have helped me on my way to accomplishing many goals.

It all began when I started to use affirmations to improve my confidence levels. When I started, I was 17 years old, shy, didn't find it very easy to make friends and I would as good as run from a girl! Within just a few days of using affirmations, I began to see a major difference in my thoughts, about how I saw myself, how is thought about happiness, my self-esteem, and positivity. Over the following weeks, everything changed for me and I was hooked – affirmations became my life. I was more outgoing and confident than I had ever been before, I found it easier to make friends and started socializing – and I started talking to girls!

This was just the start though and over the next 20 or so years, my day has begun, without fail, with 5 minutes of positive affirmations and, every day, the last thing at night, I repeat those affirmations into the bathroom mirror. Not a day has passed when I have not done this and the transformation has been remarkable.

What did I use affirmations for? Just about anything you can think of. They helped me to lose weight and start taking exercise on a regular basis. They pushed me into working hard at running and at sports. I used them to help me in my hobbies, to boost myself when I was down and to get the right mindset for running my real estate properties and my businesses. I also used them as a way of helping to boost my personal relationships and live life.

After spending the last 20 or so years running my own businesses I have now been able to take early retirement although I do keep my hand in with some business interests and personal projects. And I still do my affirmations, every single morning and night. Throughout my life, throughout all the changes, the ups, the downs, affirmations have been there for me and they can be there for you too.

Chapter 3: Phase Two – Days Nine Through Fourteen

"Thousands of candles can be lighted from a single candle, and the life of the candle will not be shortened. Happiness never decreases by being shared." – Buddha

You've made it to phase two! How did you do over the last week? Take a moment to consider how you did with the first challenge so far. Do you feel that starting your day with a quote and affirmation changed how you approached your day? Consider how you are feeling on a daily basis. Would you say that you can feel yourself becoming progressively more positive?

At this point, getting up a little earlier each day should be becoming a habit and a normal part of your routine. Remember that you are going to continue getting up early and committing that time to reflecting on the quote and daily affirmation of the day throughout the rest of the thirty days. You should also have a few affirmations that mean something to you that you are saying each day.

This phase's challenge is based on the quote above. Sharing happiness is a great way to bring more happiness to you, and when you see yourself bring happiness to others, you will be amazed at how great it makes you feel.

Challenge – Phase Two: Your challenge this phase is to spread a little happiness every day. This can mean anything you want it to. You can take a minute out of your day to call someone who you know would appreciate hearing from you. You can take a minute to thank the grocery store clerk for being kind. It could also mean surprising someone with a cup of coffee or a treat. Any form of gratitude or positivity is going to go a long way towards bringing happiness into other people's lives. When you see how happy you can make others, you are going to feel happier as well.

The reason that you feel happy when you make other people happy is that we have the ability to empathize the emotions that we observe in others. In the 1960's a Dutch Scientist, Christian Huygens discovered that if he hung multiple pendulums on the wall, they would all end up swinging in perfect synchrony. This proved to be true even if he set them in motion at different times. This happens in human beings as well. You have probably noticed that when someone is in a bad mood, that bad mood can be passed on to others. The same is true for happiness.

Day Nine

Quote: "There is only one way to happiness, and that is to cease worrying about things which are beyond the power of our will." – Epictetus

Affirmation: Happiness is my birthright. I choose to be happy, and I deserve to be happy.

Some Things You Should Consider:

While you are thinking about the quote above, consider all of the things that you are worrying about that are sacrificing your happiness. Is there anything you can do to control those things? Or are they beyond your control? For the things that are beyond your control, consider what you can do help reduce your worry about the things that are beyond your control.

Anytime you come across a situation that is decreasing your happiness, repeat the affirmation above. Remember, you deserve to be happy, and you can make the choice to be happy.

Day Ten

Quote: "It's not the events of our lives that shape us, but our beliefs as to what those events mean." – Tony Robbins

Affirmation: I always spot opportunities and utilize them. New doors are always opening for me.

Some Things You Should Consider:

Reading the above quote, can you think of some times in your life when you felt that you were being shaped by the things that were happening around you? What was shaping you, was it the event itself or how you were reacting to the event?

Many people consider themselves to be a victim of circumstance when it is an internal decision to allow the circumstance to define them. How can you change how you are viewing those circumstances?

The above affirmation is a great one when you feel as though you are being limited by your circumstances. New opportunities are always opening themselves up to you, and there are always new opportunities for you to explore.

Day Eleven

Quote: "Action is the foundational key to all success" – Pablo Picasso

Affirmation: I am solution oriented. All problems are solvable.

Some Things You Should Consider:

When you consider the quote above, remember that the foundation of anything is the most important thing. When you are building a house, the house is only as strong as the foundation. The quote tells us that actions are the foundation for success. If you aren't taking any action, you aren't going to accomplish any success.

If you have felt as though you are stuck in a rut recently, and feel as though there is no way to move forward in your life, this affirmation is exactly what you are going to need to help you through it. Repeat this affirmation to yourself as often as you can. Remember, if you are looking for the solution, you are going to find it.

Day Twelve

Quote: "Optimism is the faith that leads to achievement. Nothing can be done without hope and confidence." – Helen Keller

Affirmation: I am confident, and I am capable. There is no challenge I cannot overcome.

Some Things You Should Consider:

Think about the situations that you are the most optimistic. What are the times that you are the most confident that you are going to be able to achieve your goals? What situations are you the least confident in?

Whenever you are in doubt of your abilities, repeat the affirmation above. Place it next to your bathroom mirror, seeing it on a regular basis is going to help you believe it even more. Of all of the affirmations that we have gone over this far, this is the one that you need to believe in the most.

Day Thirteen

Quote: "To carry a positive action, we must develop here a positive vision – Dalai Lama

Affirmation: I am going to help others. I have enough happiness inside me to share.

Some Things You Should Consider:

When you read the quote above, what is the very first thought that comes to your mind? Can you think of a time when you were expecting a negative outcome and it came true? What about a time when you were expecting a positive vision and the positive vision can true? Often, when you can envision the outcome being positive, you are more likely to get that positive outcome.

People often expect the worst in a situation and tell themselves that they are expecting the worst, so they aren't disappointed when it happens. However, they are still just as disappointed when their negative vision comes to fruition. Don't get caught up in this trap. When you think negative things are going to happen, they are more likely to happen.

How are you doing on this phases' challenge? Are you finding it easy to bring happiness into other people's lives? If you are finding the challenge to be difficult, repeat the above affirmation to yourself. There is happiness inside you, and when you choose to share it with others, it comes back to you tenfold.

Day Fourteen

Quote: "You'll never find a rainbow if you're looking down" — Charlie Chaplin

Affirmation: I am kind, I am loving, I am happy.

Some Things You Should Consider:

Take time to think about what the quote above means. Think about a goal that you are trying to reach. Are you on the right path to meet that goal? If you aren't on the right path to reach your goals, you are never going to get to them. Take some time to analyze where you are in life and where you want to go. What changes can you make?

No matter how far you are from the path you want to be on, you can still be happy with where you are. Remind yourself that you are a kind and loving person. Happiness is a choice you can make. If you aren't happy at this moment, only you can change that. Repeat the affirmation above and remind yourself of all of the reasons you have to be happy.

Success Story – Whitney

"All is well. Everything is working out for my highest good. Out of this situation only good will come. I am safe." – Louise L. Hay

My name is Whitney and, in the middle of the eighties, I was given a book, a book that I still have to this day. My parents had been divorced for a few years and, although things were good, it was tough at a time when divorce want really all that common. A friend of my mother gave me this book, the Rainbow Heart Book, called "You Can heal Your Life" by Louse L Hay. And I have to say that, since that time, my life has been one hell of a journey!

This brand new book seemed to fit with me, being the kid of divorced parents at my school. Every exercise that was in it, I savored, just to get to know every different aspect of the me that I am. I wanted to be a better person, more accepting, more whole and I learned that I was a loving person, a lovable person and that I was loved, not just by me but by the entire universe – and I still am to this day.

Out of all of the techniques in this book, the one that inspired me the most and has stuck with me is affirmations. It is these that I thank for the fact that I became a happy teenager, a confident one, one who was happy to be herself and not trying to be something others wanted me to be.

For me, an affirmation is everything and anything that I think, that I say, that I believe, experience and feel. Affirmations have become me, they reflect me and they are me.

So many people use negative self-talk and this is what drives their affirmations, drawing them into negativity that they really didn't want. It started like this for me but I learned to move my focus and use my affirmations for a more positive life and it is these positive affirmations that have seen me through many an uphill struggle.

When I was in my twenties, my dad passed on, completely unexpectedly and that changed my whole life forever. I got stuck in a grief rut – Í release myself as I do in each moment, free of self-judgment"

Later on in my twenties I was diagnosed with cancer and, as it does with just about everyone who is diagnosed, it stole my breath, it stunned me. I stumbled through wondering why this was happening, what had I done? At this point, my affirmations became passionate – "I am living my life to the full, treasuring every single day as it comes"

When I was in my thirties, I became unfulfilled with my job, I wasn't happy or satisfied with what I was doing. I felt as if I was overworked, ill because of stress and burned out. My affirmations changed – Í am living my purpose in life, engaging my Sacred Gifts for the healthy benefit of me and others around me"

Today, I am that happy smiling person I was back in twelfth grade and I put that down to my belief in affirmations and the fact that I have made them a part of my daily life, especially the most important one of all – "I am truly grateful"

Chapter 4: Phase Three – Days Fifteen Through Twenty-Two

"You cannot change what happens to you but you can control your attitude towards what happens to you, and in that, you will be mastering change rather than allowing it to master you." – Brian Tracy

You are still coming back every day and reading another page in this book, and you have made it to phase three.

How do you feel you did with making other people happy in the last phase? Did you notice that making other people happy had the power to increase how you were feeling? I encourage you to continue to go out of your way to do things for others that are going to make them happy, even though it is no longer a part of your challenge.

This week's challenge is a little different than the last two weeks. This week your challenge is going to be about change. You've already been working on changing your mindset and your attitude, even if you didn't realize you were. This week we are going to take that one step further. This challenge is also going to give you a lead into your week four challenge.

Challenge – Phase Three: Your challenge this phase is going to center around making changes. For each day this phase, you are going to make a list of something good that happened, something bad that happened, and something positive that can come from the bad thing that happened. Finding something positive out of a negative is a difficult challenge, but it is an important part of finding success and happiness.

Don't worry; I am not going to send you into this challenge without any education on how you can best find the positive in a negative situation. Here are some tips to help you with this process:

1. Identify Your Emotions – If you can label the emotion you are feeling in a negative situation; you can get a better handle on the situation as a whole. This is because you will be able to tell what emotions are skewing your interpretation of the situation.

2. Find A Lesson – There is a lesson in every situation. If you work hard to find the lesson, you are more likely to see the positive in a situation.

3. Look For The Benefit – Sometimes when you find yourself in a negative situation, there is something small that you are going to gain a benefit. This could be something like a free cup of coffee after receiving the wrong order at the coffee shop or trying a new dish when the restaurant ran out of an ingredient that is necessary for your usual. In both of these situations you can choose to dwell on the negative aspect of the situation, and indeed, they would seem to be a big deal to some people. However, you also have the choice to focus on the compensation the coffee shop gave you or the fantastic new dish you experienced.

Use these tips to help you change the view of some of your experiences this week from negative to positive.

Day Fifteen

Quote: "To create more positive results in your life, replace 'if only' with 'next time'." – Celestine Chua

Affirmation: There is a great reason this is unfolding before me now.

Some Things You Should Consider:

When things aren't going the way you want them to in your life, think about how you typically respond. If you find that you are often responding in a helpless manner, this quote is exactly what you need to think about. Instead of feeling helpless, consider the things you would do differently if you were in the same situation again.

The affirmation above is great for reminding you that everything happens for a reason. Sometimes that reason is clear and other times it isn't. When you feel like you aren't able to identify the reason that something in your life is happening, repeat this quote to yourself as often as you can until you have been able to find positive reasons for the situation.

Day Sixteen

Quote: "A pessimist sees the difficulty in every opportunity; an optimist sees the opportunity in every difficulty" – Winston Churchill

Affirmation: I can overcome this challenge. This challenge is going to lead to great things for me.

Some Things You Should Consider:

Reading the quote, try to determine if you are more of an optimist or a pessimist. Keep in mind; it is possible to be both an optimist and a pessimist depending on the situation that you find yourself in.

Think about the situations that you find yourself to be pessimistic in. In those situations, is it possible for you to find something positive that you can focus on?

When you find yourself in a position that it is hard to see the positive in, use the affirmation above to remind yourself that you can overcome any challenges and challenges are meant to lead you to new opportunities, as long as you are open to seeing them.

Day Seventeen

Quote: "We become what we think about" – Earl Nightingale

Affirmation: I am capable of seeing the good in every situation. I am defined by the things I choose to think about.

Some Things You Should Consider:

We have already discussed that your frame of mind is a huge part of what goes on around you, or at least how you perceive it. When considering the quote above, "We become what we think about," think about the strengths you have and the strengths you would like to have. Think about a negative situation you have been in lately, what good was in that situation?

Using the affirmation above, remind yourself that there is good in every situation, regardless of how negative it seems like the time. Negative situations do not have the ability to define you. Choose to see, and focus, on whatever good you can find in a moment, even if it isn't directly related to the situation.

Day Eighteen

Quote: "Find a place inside where there's joy, and the joy will burn out the pain" – Joseph Campbell

Affirmation: My body is healthy; my mind is brilliant; my soul is tranquil.

Some Things You Should Consider:

Sometimes it can seem as if all of the negativity around you is bringing you down and you can't bring yourself above it all. The quote above is a reminder to find the joy that is inside you, regardless of what it is you feel joy about, and allow the joy to outshine the negativity all around you.

The affirmation above serves as a reminder that there is always something to be thankful for. Having gratitude for your body, mind, and soul is a great way to show joy and to allow that joy to become your primary focus.

Day Nineteen

Quote*:* "Our greatest weakness lies in giving up. The most certain way to succeed is always to try just one more time." – Thomas A. Edison

Affirmation*:* I see the perfection in all my flaws and all my genius.

Some Things You Should Consider:

Think about the quote above. Can you think of a time that you gave up? What about a situation where you decided to try one more time and that last try was the difference between finding success and being unsuccessful? While it is important to know when to approach a situation from a different angle or to leave a situation and focus your efforts elsewhere, if there is something you truly want the only way you are going to get it is to keep trying.

Every part of you is important to who you are. This includes your strengths and your weaknesses. If you try to hide your flaws and only show your strengths, you are not going to be happy, and people aren't going to know you for the real you. Embrace your flaws and weaknesses as a crucial part of your personality. Use the affirmation above to remind yourself that your flaws aren't necessarily a bad thing, and can be used to your advantage.

Day Twenty

Quote: "Believe that your life is worth living, and your belief will help create the fact" – William James

Affirmation: I am worth having good things happen to me. I bring happiness into my life.

Some Things You Should Consider:

Do you genuinely feel that your life is worth living? Do you feel like you are making a significant contribution to society, or at the very least to the people who are closest to you?

By using the affirmation above, you can remind yourself that you are worth having good things happening. No one is inherently deserving of having bad things happen to them. The things that happen to us are the things that we have brought into our lives. Remind yourself that you are worth being happiness and that good things can happen to you too, and then look for those good things to begin happening.

Day Twenty-One

Quote: "You can always do more than you think you can" – John Wooden

Affirmation: I am capable of accomplishing whatever I set my mind to.

Some Things You Should Consider:

The quote above serves as a reminder that we all tend to undersell ourselves, especially to ourselves. Think about a time when you gave up on something because you felt as though you weren't able to do what you had originally set out to do. Or, perhaps a time when you only did the bare minimum because you didn't feel like you were able to contribute anything extra to a project. Now think about a time when you pushed yourself further than you thought you were capable of being pushed. How did you feel afterward?

Use the affirmation above as often as you can. This is another great affirmation to ensure that you put somewhere that you can see it constantly throughout the day. Reminding yourself that you are capable of accomplishing anything you want to is an important part of learning how to push yourself out of your comfort zone and into a position of learning more about yourself.

Day Twenty-Two

Quote: "Very little is needed to make a happy life; it is all within yourself, in your way of thinking." – Marcus Aurelius

Affirmation: My life is fulfilling and makes me happy.

Some Things You Should Consider:

You are the master of your happiness. No one can determine whether or not you are happy except you. You make the choice regarding how you are going to react to a situation. Think about a time when you were in a negative situation, but you remained happy overall and didn't let the situation ruin your entire day or your entire week.

The quote above is one that is great for every person in the world to remember. If you can, place this quote somewhere permanent. Somewhere you are going to see it in the morning when you wake up, throughout the day and again in the evening. Telling yourself that your life is fulfilling is the first step in believing your life is fulfilling.

Success Story – Donna

"What God says you are is more important than what others think of you."

— *Lailah Gifty Akita*

My name is Donna and I have to tell you, I am dead excited about affirmations. I follow the Christian faith and I always had it in my head that affirmations were nothing more than New-Age nonsense but I'm here to tell you that they are not and I have found them so incredibly useful.

Most of us watch the Olympics when it's on the TV. I watched the recent Winter Olympics because it gives me inspiration. I see people who have found true success at what they do, people who compete to be the top of their field, their game. They are incredibly focused on what they are doing and, to get to where they are, they have spent virtually every day working towards their goal, preparing themselves and taking part in all the major competitions and other events that happen along the way. They have succeeded at all these events and now they are at the Olympics, champions.

There is one thing that stands out with all of these athletes; before they compete in their event, they close their eyes and rehearse what they are going to do in their minds. They visualize themselves skiing down the slope, racing that course; they rehearse the routines that they have done so many times before and they feel their muscles working those movements They see it all happening and that happens because they think about it and they practice repeatedly.

I used to play the violin professionally and would practice for a minimum of 5 hours every single day, as well as taking part in rehearsals. It seemed I would always be preparing myself, practicing for a concert and I always had a deadline to work to. I had a specific goal in mind, either of being the best musician I could be or of joining a violinist group and performing with them. When I wasn't physically practicing, I would be mentally practicing.

Affirmations are exactly the same. I asked myself some questions – "where do I want to be in 5 years?", how healthy do I want to be?", "How successful do I want to be?" and a whole host of other similar questions. Then I asked myself what I should do NOW to get to where I wanted to be in 5 years' time. I never once said to myself that I couldn't achieve it. Instead, I told myself that to be successful, I needed to certain things, the same way that every successful person does. If a successful person got there by eating food that was raw and living and drinking only green tea, then that is what I had to do. If I wanted the same success I had to do the same things.

My next step was to come up with an action plan, a schedule that included all of these activities I needed to do on a daily basis. I kept saying to myself the affirmation, "successful people do ABC and because I am a successful person, I must also do ABC". It really didn't take long for everything to fall into place!

My daily affirmations are extremely simple. I say them every morning and I say them every night before I go to bed. I also say them throughout the day as well. I am fighting a disease called muscular dystrophy so one of my daily affirmations is, "I am a very powerful and strong woman". My spirit and my mind tell me it is true and I know that the more I say this affirmation, the more my cells will understand that it is true. Already, I am able to move in ways that I couldn't do several weeks ago.

One thing I do have to be careful of is thought processes and attitude. It is very easy to get wound up in negative thinking, such as, "I am never going to be well again, I will never make a good marriage/mother/wife, I will never have plenty of money" and things like that. But, by using positive affirmations every day, and pushing the negative ones out of my life, I can truly say that my life has changed so much and all of it for the better.

I can see the changes happening in my mind and I keep an eye on the daily actions that I do to make sure I am continually moving forwards, toward my personal goals and not away from them. I write down small goals that are achievable so that I can see them in black and white. This makes me more likely to do them and I will repeat my positive affirmations, stop negative thoughts from forming and it truly works.

A positive affirmation is saying something to yourself that you deeply believe to be true or what you would like to be true; it is in effect, putting faith into action. If you read a passage in the bible that says, "I want nothing more than to see you prosper and be in health" then it is perfectly fine for your affirmation to be, "I am prosperous and healthy, by my faith."

Chapter 5: Phase Four – Days Twenty-Three Through Thirty

*"Keep your thoughts positive, because your thoughts become your words.
Keep your words positive, because your words become your behavior.
Keep your behavior positive, because your behavior becomes your habits.
Keep your habits positive, because your habits become your values.
Keep your values positive, because your values become your destiny."* – Mahatma Gandhi

You have made it through the first three phases of this book. Let's take a minute and analyze how your thoughts have changed while you have been reading this book. Consider how much happier you are feeling. Think about your levels of optimism when you are facing a difficult situation. Analyze how easily you are conceding defeat and how much harder you are trying to meet your goals.

Another thing to consider is the challenge back from phase one. Have you still been getting up a little bit earlier in the morning to work on reading and thinking about the quotes and affirmations? Do you feel as though waking up a little bit earlier has become a routine now? Think about how you feel after reading the quotes and affirmations. Are you finding yourself looking forward to seeing what the next day has in store for you? Consider if your days are feeling more positive after reading your daily quote and affirmation.

This phase is going to be set up a little bit differently than the last three phases were. Over the last twenty-two days, I have given you both the quote and the affirmation for you to think about and apply to your life. While I am still going to give you the quote each day, this week's challenge is going to require you to come up with your affirmations that are more personal to you.

Challenge – Phase Four: Coming up with your affirmations isn't going to be difficult. By coming up with your affirmations, they are going to be more meaningful and powerful in your life and your situation. The reason they are more powerful is that they are personalized to your life and your way of thinking. When you use a personalized affirmation instead of one that is generic and not geared to your specific situation it becomes something that you own and that you know geared towards making your life better. This is going to enable you to feel more connected to the words.

You are not going to be alone in this challenge. Each day I am going to guide you through the process of creating your affirmation, working off the quotes that have been included.

I am going to guide you through the creation of the affirmation to be sure that you are creating effective affirmations that are going to genuinely benefit your life. Affirmations that don't benefit you are useless. If at any time you find that a particular affirmation is no longer useful to you, switch it out with something else that is of use to you and your life.

How To Write An Effective Affirmation:

Before we move on and have you writing your affirmations, here is a quick outline of what an effective affirmation needs to contain.

- Write an affirmation that is a positive spin on a negative thought or situation. The language you are using is incredibly important. You want to write an affirmation that is going to resonate with you on a personal level.

- Write in the present tense as often as you can. While writing affirmations in the future tense can be acceptable sometimes, it makes it sound as though it is a goal you are going to reach for in the future instead of something you want to see in your life right now. When you have a goal that you are going to work towards sometime in the future, it is not an effective goal, and the same is true for affirmations.

- Avoid words that elicit judgment. Words like never and always are very strong and judgmental words. You want your affirmation to be gentle and bring relief from judgments.

- Make your affirmations personal. Use the pronouns 'I' and 'My' in your affirmations to raise the level of commitment and belief you are going to have in the affirmation.

Day Twenty-Three

Quote: "Success is not final; failure is not fatal: it is the courage to continue that counts" – Winston Churchill

Affirmation:

To create your affirmation today, think of something that you are currently working on that you feel as though you should quit. This can be something big like a job, or relationship, or it could be something small like a goal to go to the gym or read a different book each month. Choose something that you feel like you aren't successful at, but you also don't want to quit. Avoid choosing something like smoking, as that isn't going to fit into this style of affirmation.

Think back over some of the affirmations that you have used over the last few weeks. Many of them had a similar theme to them but were not personal to your situation. Instead, they were generic and able to be used by many different people in different situations.

Write one that is personal to the situation you chose above.

I am going to provide you with some examples as we go through this chapter and for each one I am going to relate them to a runner who is very committed to becoming a better runner but is thinking about giving up because he hasn't successfully run five miles. An example of his affirmation could be: "I am strong enough to go to the gym. I have the stamina to run five miles."

Remember to use only positive words. Using something like "I am not too tired to go to the gym" is not going to be as effective as "I have the energy to go to the gym."

Day Twenty-Four

Quote: "Getting over a painful experience is much like crossing monkey bars. You have to let go at some point to move forward." – Clive S. Lewis

Affirmation:

We have all gone through painful experiences in our lifetime. Sometimes we can let them go and move on and other times we hold onto those things and let them determine where our lives are going.

Think about something you failed at that you haven't tried to do again because you failed. This can be as big or small as you would like it to be. Remember, starting with something that is small and insignificant isn't going to produce the same results as starting with something meaningful.

Here is an example using the runner I used yesterday. Let's say our runner went to the gym and practiced every day and signed up for a five-mile marathon, but after four miles broke his ankle in three places and needed a lot of rehabilitation before he could even attempt to walk again, never mind run. He could give up on running, which would be pretty easy. Or, he could use an affirmation like this: "My body is strong. I will begin running again."

Using an affirmation like this is going to out the runner into the mindset not to give up and to let go of the fall he had and keep focusing on moving forwards.

Just like yesterday, keep the affirmation positive and don't use any words that have a negative connotation. Negative words tend to stick in your brain as negative words, even if used in a positive way.

Day Twenty-Five

Quote: "Life's most persistent and urgent question is, "what are you doing for others?" – Martin Luther King, Jr.

Affirmation:

A couple of phases ago, your challenge was to spread happiness to at least one person every day. Were you successful in that challenge? Did you continue going out of your way to make people happy as the days progressed? Today's affirmation is going to be about what you do for the people around you on a regular basis. Consider how much you donate. Whether it is donating your time volunteering, your money or your old belongings, do you believe you are doing everything you can do to help other people?

We are going to use the same runner that we have been using previously for our examples. We know that he is a good runner, and now he wants to help people out with his skills. His affirmation may look something like this: "I can raise awareness of safety while running." Or "I am going to talk to people about overcoming obstacles and not giving up on themselves." This demonstrates that the runner is using his experiences to educate others.

Think about things you are able to do that would help someone else. This affirmation doesn't need to be as specific as "I am going to help Susie with her homework." It can be something like "I am going to donate my time to (a cause that is important to you)" Remember, don't just say it. Act on your affirmation as well. Following through on your affirmation is just as important as creating your affirmation.

Day Twenty-Six

Quote: "Do not dwell in the past, do not dream of the future, concentrate the mind on the present moment" – Buddha

Affirmation:

Do you know what it means to be mindful? Being mindful means that you are present in each moment. The quote above sums it up completely - avoid dwelling on the past and the future and focus on the present moment that you are living. Notice all of the small things that are happening around. Don't get so caught up in thinking about how your day at work was, or the project that you have due tomorrow that you miss all the little things going on at this moment.

Think about your personal life. Where do your thoughts tend to dwell? Consider if you are constantly stuck in the past or if you are more concerned about where your future is going to bring you.

Our runner is focused on running in the next marathon. Because of this focus, he tends to forget his commitments to his family, and this creates a lot of tension. Some of his affirmations may include:

- "I have the focus to be present in the moment."
- "The future will take care of itself. My family is more important than running."
- "I can be present in the moment and be a good runner."

Think about people who are close to you that may feel as though you are always distracted. If this affirmation is harder to write up, consider asking those who are closest to you if they feel like you give them your undivided attention.

Day Twenty-Seven

Quote*:* "In the long run the pessimist may be proved right, but the optimist has a better time on the trip." – Daniel L. Reardon

Affirmation:

We have spent a lot of time analyzing optimism and pessimism, and you should be able to identify which of the two categories you fall into. We have also looked at a couple of different quotes about enjoying the moment instead of focusing on only where we want to go. While that is the main focus of this quote, I want you to take your affirmation in a slightly different direction.

Last week your challenge was to make a list of negative situations and something positive that came out of it. Today you are going to come up with three things about yourself that you don't like, and you are going to spin them into positive affirmations.

For example; Our runner suffers from insomnia, he feels that he is always snapping at his children, and he never makes time for his wife. His affirmations would look like this:

- "I am completely free from insomnia." While this isn't yet true, by telling himself over and over again that it is true, he is going to bring the relief from insomnia into his life.

- "It is deeply satisfying for me to respond with wisdom, love, firmness, and self-control when my children misbehave." By reminding himself how he should respond to his children, he is more likely to respond the way he wants to.

- "It is important to me to spend time with my wife on a daily basis. I love my wife and want to see her happy." Using this affirmation is going to make his wife more important to our runner and is going to make spending time with her a priority.

Come up with three or more affirmations for yourself that are specific to things about you or your life that you are unhappy with. Try to make these three affirmations ones that you would want to be saying every day.

Day Twenty-Eight

Quote: "To change your life, you have to change yourself. To change yourself you have to change your mindset." – Wilson Kanadi

Affirmation:

Changing your mindset is not an easy thing to do, but if you want to see some real changes in your life, you need to change how you are looking at things. As we are coming to the end of our thirty days together, it is vital that you are able to keep up the changes that you have begun making. That is the purpose behind today's affirmation.

To create today's affirmation, you are going to consider what your biggest obstacles in doing the challenges in this book have been. Perhaps you have struggled with making time each day to sit and read and think about the quote and affirmation. Maybe you found that you had a hard time saying the affirmations out loud and believing in them. Or, perhaps it was acknowledging your flaws that you have the hardest time with. Whatever it was that you had a hard time with, use all of the knowledge you have about affirmations to create an affirmation to counter whatever your biggest struggle may be.

Day Twenty-Nine

Quote: "Most of the important things in the world have been accomplished by people who had kept on trying when there seemed no hope at all." – Dale Carnegie

Affirmation:

Sometimes we hit a point in our lives where things seem hopeless. Chances are, you have been there before, and you will experience that again. Today we are going to create an affirmation for a time when things are feeling hopeless. Even if you aren't in a hopeless situation right now, it is important to have an affirmation that is going to allow you to boost yourself up. This is both to avoid a hopeless situation and to help you out of it if you find yourself in a hopeless situation.

Think about a time when you have felt hopeless in the past. What is something someone said to you that helped you, or something you wish someone had said to you?

We are going to go back to our runner to demonstrate an example. Our runner is getting ready to run an eight-mile marathon. The marathon states that the eight miles must be completed in forty minutes in order to earn a medal. Our runner desperately wants this medal, but the best time he can get is fifty minutes, and he feels hopeless. Here are a couple of affirmations he could use:

- "I can run eight miles in forty minutes."
- "I am a successful runner; I have earned my times."
- "My family loves me, and I am a great person just the way I am."

As you can see, the third example is a little more generic than the first two. While you want to be as specific as possible, sometimes an affirmation that leans towards being generic is helpful as you can apply it to more aspects of your life. If this is an affirmation you are going to keep in your reserves for when you need it, a generic affirmation can be altered to match a situation later, when the situation presents itself.

Day Thirty

Quote: "Why Worry? If you've done the very best you can, worrying won't make it any better" – Walt Disney

Affirmation:

Knowing that you have done the best you can in any situation is an important part of being at peace with the decisions you have made and the outcomes of those decisions. As we end this book, you may be worried about moving into using affirmations on your own. Don't be. By doing the best you could throughout this book, you have undergone a transformation in your thinking, and you are now ready to move forward on your own.

Worrying about what is going to happen next is something that we are all guilty of, but doesn't accomplish anything. Instead of requiring you to create your affirmation today, I am going to give you five affirmations that are about not worrying. I want you to read through them and choose the one that you feel is the most natural for you to say. Take this affirmation and change the words to make it personal and about you.

- "I am letting go of my worries."
- "I am able to solve problems and worries using logic."
- "I will be relaxed and calm."
- "I am a naturally calm person."
- "I am confident and at peace with my life right now."

Success Story – Karen

"If you are determined to achieve your dreams, you must be ready to accept and affirm positive things about yourself. Affirm positively! Say positive things and encourage yourself that you can make it." – Israelmore Ayivor

My name is Karen and I want to tell you about my personal experience with affirmations. Recently, I learned a great deal about using affirmations to lose weight, about how it worked and now I want to share my experiences with you.

My whole life has been about one big search. I always had it in my mind that there was something terribly important that we had all forgotten, something about living how we do on earth and I have always believed that we the human race, are far powerful than we ever knew.

One way or another, I have been on this diet or that one ever since I was a teenager. I am now in my middle fifties. When I diet these days, no matter what I do, no matter how much I restrict what I eat, nothing happens. I can, however, put weight on easily when I eat normally.

I decided that I needed to change the way I was thinking, to start thinking positive things about losing weight. What else did I have to lose? Diets weren't working anymore so the very first thing I thought was that I was never going to go on another diet again. And it is to this that I attribute the success of my affirmations. When you think about it, the act of dieting actually causes a feeling of lacking. I firmly believe that your unconsciousness believes that you are starving when you go on a diet and, as such, it holds on fast to all that stored fat so that, when you "starve" yourself again, it can feed you and keep you alive. It is also this very thing that causes you to gain every single pound of fat back; it has absolutely no consideration of the good or the bad about losing weight.

Recently, I put on weight, about 8 lbs. so I changed my affirmation. I said to myself, *"I am .... lbs."*. I made it 8 lbs. lower than what I weighed and I said it every single night before I went to bed, as well as every single morning when I got up. However, it was also a mantra that I repeated through the course of the day and during the night if I woke. Two weeks later, I weighed myself; nothing had changed. After three weeks, those 8 lbs. had disappeared.

When I tried this gain, I lowered my affirmation weight by 10 lbs. and kept repeating my affirmation every day for two months. Nothing happened so I thought it must have been a fluke the first time around. I tried again but this time reducing my weight but just 5 lbs. It did work but it took a month. I tried again with the 5 lbs. reduction but this time, I was able to repeat the affirmation much more than I could before and it only took two weeks to work this time.

This month, I am concentrating on other things but I will return to my weight loss soon. What is interesting this time is that, no matter what I eat, I have neither gained any weight nor lost it. It would appear that my unconscious is under the belief that I will weight whatever my last affirmation was, no matter what I do, or until I tell it otherwise.

I hope this will encourage you to give affirmations a try. You do need to be able to stick to it and push on even though you may want to give but it will work; it did for me where nothing else would.

Chapter 6: What if it Doesn't Work?

Muhammad Ali had one affirmation that he used to repeat, over and over again, until he became the words he spoke – *"I AM THE GREATEST"*

Provided they are used properly, affirmations have been scientifically proven to be a truly effective means of becoming who you want to be, the person you must become to achieve all that you want to achieve throughout life. However, affirmations have also been given something of a bad time because many people have tried them and have failed to achieve what they want.

The reason they have failed is because things have changed. For many decades, so-called gurus and experts told us that we should be doing affirmations in a specific way, a way that is destined to be completely ineffective and will only cause failure, no matter how much you try them. There are two problems here:

First off, if you lie to yourself, it simply won't work. Saying things like:

"I am a millionaire" when you clearly aren't

"My body fat is only 7%" when it most certainly isn't

"I have achieved every goal I set for myself in the last year" when you really haven't

All of this is going to fail because you are lying to yourself. This way of saying affirmations, as if you have already achieved something or become something you aren't is the biggest single reason for failure. If you use this technique, every time you speak an affirmation that isn't based firmly in truth, your unconscious will kick it aside because it knows it isn't true. You are an intelligent person and repeatedly lying to yourself will never work simply because the truth will always come out.

Let's take an affirmation like, *"I am a magnet for money; money comes to me in vast amounts without any effort"*; this might make you feel fantastic while you are saying it because it takes away from your very real worries about finances but it will never ever result in income. Anyone who sits and waits for money to come to them without doing anything to make it happen will always be cash poor.

If you want to generate money in abundance, or anything else that you desire, you do actually have to do something to make it happen. Every action you take must be aligned with the results that you want to achieve and affirmations must both state and affirm both parts of that.

The following are four steps that will help you to create affirmations that you can implement, affirmations that will go into your conscious mind and your subconscious to produce the results that you want for success beyond what you thought possible before.

Each and every affirmation must be created in this way:

Step 1 – The Result That You Are Committed to Achieving and Why

Note that you are not beginning with something that you WANT. We all want something but we don't always get what we want. Instead, we only get what we are committed to achieving. So you want to be a millionaire; don't we all so come and join this club that is not exclusive. Oh, hold on, you are committed to becoming a millionaire, 100% committed and you will do whatever is necessary, the actions that you need to take to achieve that result. Now, we're on the right track.

Action - write down one very specific and extraordinary result that you are committed to achieving. Choose one that is going to challenge you and will make significant improvements to your life; improvements that you are 100% ready to commit to making. It doesn't matter yet that you don't know how you will achieve this, that will come later. Next, your affirmation must contain a reason why you are going to do this, compelling reasons and the benefit that you will get from it.

Examples

Here are some examples of affirmations written in this way:

" I am committed to increasing my income in the next year from $... to $... so that I can give my family financial security."

"I am committed 100% to losing ...lbs. and weighing ...lbs. by (input a specific date) so that I can set the right example for my children/decrease my risks of serious disease."

Step 2 – The Actions You Commit to Taking and When

It would be easy to write down an affirmation that merely says what you want without saying what you are going to do but this would be as good as pointless. In actual fact, it could be seen as being counter-productive because all you are doing is telling your subconscious that you can achieve the result without doing anything.

Action – Clarify exactly what you are going to do to achieve the result you want, be it an activity, an action or a habit that needs to be changed if you are going to be successful.

State clearly when you will do this and how often you must do in order to achieve the necessary action.

Examples:

"To ensure that I increase my income, I am 100% committed to making 40 prospecting calls every day, between 8 am and 10 am, no matter what happens.

"To make sure I lose …lbs., I am committed 100% to attending the gym every day and running for at least 20 minutes a day on the treadmill between 6 am and 7 am".

If you make your actions specific, the better they will be. Make sure that you include how often, how many and specific time frames.

Step 3 – Repeat Your Affirmation Each Morning with Emotion

Remember this; these affirmations are designed purely to make you feel better. These are statements that you have written, statements that have been engineered to program your mindset and beliefs into your subconscious so that you are able to achieve the outcome you want. At the same time, they will be telling your conscious mind that you need to remain focused on high priorities and carry out the actions that are going to get you to the end of your journey.

That said, if your affirmations are going to be effective, you have to use emotion when you are saying them. If you repeat your affirmation over and over without feeling the truth of it, it won't work or at best, you will only get mediocre results. It is your responsibility to generate real excitement and real determination and then bring those emotions into each of your affirmations, every time you say them.

Action – Set a specific time every morning to say your affirmations. The reason for this is because you have to both program the subconscious and train the conscious mind on what is truly important to you and what your commitments are to making it happen. To do this, you have to be consistent and so you have to say your affirmations at the same time every single day. Once you make these a solid part of your routine, only then will you see the results start to happen.

Step 4 – Update Your Affirmations and Evolve Them Constantly

As your commitments begin to be realized, you will improve and evolve and, because of that, your affirmations must do the same. Once you reach a goal, set up a new one and add it to your affirmation. You can have an affirmation for every part of your life that is significant – your health, finances, family, relationships, etc. – and you should evolve your affirmations on a constant basis as your learning increases.

In the next few chapters, I am going to give you some positive affirmations to say for three different areas of your life – success, health, and career, followed by some motivational ones and then I will be showing you some techniques on learning how to write and use your own affirmations. Once you have completed the 30-day course, don't stop. Pick any of these affirmations or write your own and continue reaping the success that you have already experienced.

Chapter 7: Positive Affirmations for Success

Breathe in deeply a couple of times and clear out your mind – you do not need any distractions at this point. When you read these affirmations, read them with true meaning and really feel the meaning of each one deep inside of you. Repeat each one as many times as necessary until you really feel it, in your bones and in your heart.

Smile widely and make it a genuine smile and then read each of them aloud. If you need help in truly feeling the power of each one, don't be afraid to jump up and down, grab at the air and use your fists to pull that energy into you. Repeat them with real deep meaning to bring much faster results. This is the trick with affirmations – you have to mean them and you have to feel them.

I am always present and I am always in the moment.

I am open to receiving great quantities wealth, health, and happiness.

My life is mine to create.

I enjoy my life. It is full of beauty and abundance.

I attract everything I need to be happy, whole and healthy and I do it effortlessly.

I am consistently finding new opportunities and successes.

I live my life wholeheartedly and with passion.

My world is filled with love, beauty, happiness, and abundance.

I deserve prosperity and abundance.

I use my unique talents and gifts to manifest abundance.

I live a life full of joy and honesty.

I deserve to live a full and complete life.

I produce financial affluence by doing what I love and loving what I do.

I am surrounded by people who love me and give me support.

People recognize my existence and they appreciate it.

My love and pure zest for life motivates and inspires other people.

I share my gifts with other people generously and I accept their gifts with genuine gratitude.

I am known for my full-of-life attitude and the positive energy I give off.

I seek mentorship and inspiration from successful people that I admire.

I listen with patience, understanding and compassion to other people.

I communicate professionally, gracefully and clearly.

My success is vital.

I contribute an influential and positive presence to the world.

I celebrate life and the beauty of it every single day.

I live a full life.

I create the lifestyle I want to live with enthusiasm.

I choose success, happiness, and health.

I celebrate love, health and life itself every day.

The miracle and magic of life surround me wherever I go!

Right now, every dream I have is coming true!

And so it is.

Chapter 8: Positive Affirmations for Good Health

When you are healthy you are wealthy and positive affirmations play a huge part in this. When your mind is centered around thoughts of health, your body will follow and will be healthier. We know that there is a connection between the mind and the body and it has been agreed that some diseases are psychosomatic – caused by emotion and thought.

Even those diseases that are caused by a germ can be thought of in some way as being psychosomatic because we "allow" the germs to enter our bodies or germs that already exist there will become stronger, strong enough to cause a disease simply because your immune system is not working effectively because of emotion.

All emotion is controlled completely by thought and we all know that thought can be formed entirely at will. Positive affirmations will help to mold those thoughts and that is where the connection between these affirmations and your health become clearer.

There is an old saying, *"Change Your Thoughts, Change Your Life"* and it is perfectly possible to fill up your mind with thoughts of health just by using the right positive affirmations. Repeating them over and over again will train your subconscious mind to the extent where it begins to transform your body in line with your thoughts.

Believe it or now, and I would never make light of a subject like this, there have been cases of cancer being overcome by the power of thought. You all know about placebos and it is well known that in medical terms, the placebo effect is psychological, i.e. in your mind. A patient would be given a sugar pill instead of the real medication but would be told that it was the real thing needed to cure his condition. And in many cases, it will cure it because the patient is convinced he is taking the proper medication The placebo itself does nothing; it is all in his mind. Affirmations can have exactly the same effect on your body.

There is also evidence that different mental emotions cause different chemicals to be produced in your body. When you are feeling happy, the chemicals produced are beneficial to your body. When you are feeling sad, those chemicals are harmful to your body. As such, your thoughts effect what your body feels and does. It is very clear that positive affirmations can have very positive health effects on your body.

Below is a list of health affirmations. Choose only those that fit your situation and repeat 100 time every day for a period of 6 months. If you are on any medication that has been prescribed for your condition, DO NOT, under any circumstances, stop taking it. Affirmations are designed as a way of complementing the medication, not replacing it, and they will help to strengthen your mind, change your thought direction and assist your body in healing.

Every single day, in every single way, I am getting better and healthier

I love myself and I am healthy

Every single cell throughout my body is conscious of health. I am a health nut

My mind is perfectly calm and full of peace and my body is full of vitality and energy

I don't eat junk; I eat nutritious healthy food that is beneficial to my body and I drink large quantities of water to cleanse my system

I only think positive thoughts and I am always joyful and happy, no matter what life throws at me

I always feel great and my body feels great; I radiate positivity and happiness

Every single day is a brand new day of health, happiness, and hope

It is my birthright to be healthy. I take good care of my body and I bless it daily

I am always happy, hearty and hale. Happy in spirit, hearty in disposition and hale in body

My heart is strong and my body is steel. I am full of energy, vitality and am vigorous

Godliness is first, good health is second. I possess a healthy body and a healthy mind

With each day that passes, my body becomes healthier and full of energy

My body is a temple. It is clean, holy and good

I practice deep breathing, take regular exercise and only eat healthy nutritious foods

I am free of high/low blood pressure, I am free of diabetes and am free of any other disease that may threaten my life

I release any ill feelings I have, about anything or anyone and I forgive everyone that is associated with me

Every day, I thank God and I thank everybody in my life. I know that, without you all, I am not a complete person and I thank you for coming into and for staying in my life

My Motto is "Healthy, wealthy and wise". I have a healthy body, I have wealth and I have a wise mind

I am my creator. I am the one, I am the All

Chapter 9: Positive Affirmations for your Career

The positive career affirmations I am going to tell you will help you to see your goals, your career, your attitude and your relationships with everyone you work with or for more clearly. The definition of a career is, "a chosen pursuit, a profession or an occupation; the general course or progression of one's working life or one's professional achievements".

It is perfectly natural to want a successful career in the job or area that you choose and we all want to do a good job, to enjoy it and to earn enough money. You can choose a career in a specific job, in a specific profession or a business and it is perfectly possible to earn job satisfaction and a good reward in financial terms in any of these three areas, provided you are prepared to take the right steps necessary to ensure it.

There are lots of important things, not least knowledge in your chosen field, hard work, and proper planning, not to mention a real vision. However, more important is having the right attitude mentally. Thomas Jefferson once said, *nothing can stop the man with the right mental attitude from achieving his goal; nothing on earth can help the man with the wrong mental attitude."*

At times, we all need a good boost mentally in our work; we sometimes need to give ourselves a good talking to and this is where positive career affirmations can help you immensely. The affirmations I have listed below are going to help you get in tune with the work you do, in turn with your colleagues, your bosses, and your juniors. They will help you to get your priorities in the right order and help to focus your mind on your career.

Pick one or more from this list. You can use them on their own or you can combine them to make your own affirmations that suit your particular circumstances. Repeat your affirmations 100 times a day as a minimum, standing in front of a mirror as you say them. Over time, your mindset will change and you will become more successful in your career.

At this moment, I am working in the job of my dreams

I love my career; I get total job satisfaction from it

I love my career; It lets me grow and gives me good financial reward

I can balance my family and my career so that they work together

I am valued at my place of work and I am always listened to respectfully

I have a good relationship with my boss and all my colleagues

I am content because the work I do doesn't just benefit me; it also benefits the society that I live in

My job has fantastic career prospects, opportunities for promotion and great financial compensation

Because I have such a positive attitude mentally, I always get the best projects and the best people to help me with them

I am always full of enthusiasm and this rubs off on my colleagues, resulting in a fantastic and productive working day for everyone

I was born to be an entrepreneur. Whenever opportunities arise, I recognize then and I seize them

I am a master at sales. My customers trust me and they love me and my order book is always full to overflowing

I have a work ethic that makes sure I always get the pay raises and the promotions

My forte is my self-discipline. In my home, my family comes first and in my workplace, work comes first

I always take responsibility for my work and my actions. My work motto is, "The buck stops here".

I practice diligence in my work, honesty in my attitude and have a positive mindset at all times which opens up new opportunities for me

I look after my junior staff and I help them in the appropriate way. I am friendly toward my colleagues and show respect to my seniors

To me, a career is just the means to the end. The end is the total fulfillment of my true potential and happiness and my career gives me that every day.

I do my very best in my career every single day and I give everything with no reservations. The fruits of that labor taste very sweet

My one aim is to satisfy my customers and I always give everything to be the best that I can be and to achieve that aim

Chapter 10: Positive Affirmations for Motivation

No matter what you do in life, the most important thing is motivation. Positive motivational affirmations will give you the strength that you need to start any task and see it right through to completion. It is the motivation that allows you start that task or start any action that is needed to help you reach your goal. Without that motivation, you may start out with all the best intentions but they will soon wither away and you will give up or only do a half-hearted job.

Think of motivation as the protein that builds up the muscles and as the carbohydrate that fuels you with the energy you need to complete the task that takes you to your goal. Positive affirmations are fuel; the feed the actions and, while you can start a job or a task without any motivation, you need it to finish Repeating these affirmations regularly will provide you with an inner sense of motivation, an urge to get on and do what has to be done without any pushing and prompting, from you or from others. Your actions will be on a kind of auto-pilot until your goal is reached.

There is evidence from studies that finds we radiate those thoughts that are in our minds the most often. In turn, those thoughts will attract to you the circumstances that favor those thoughts and favor the people around you who have similar thoughts. Throughout this book, I have given you a number of quotes – don't underestimate the importance of these. They are an important resource for motivation because they tend to contain pearls of wisdom from people who are successful, whose words come from their life experiences. That makes them invaluable because there is no better teacher than life itself.

Like every other type of affirmation, a motivational affirmation is simple to prepare. Simply think about the task you are going to do and take note of the positive thoughts that enter your mind. Formulate those thoughts and include them in your affirmations, like the following examples:

I can! I can do it! I can!

When I have clear intentions, the universe will cooperate with me and I can do anything

I think only positive thoughts and only positive things are happening in my life

I am one of life's go-getters and I will do anything to achieve my goals

Success is my middle name. I am successful at everything I do

The doors that lead to opportunity are always open and I take full advantage of them with no exception

Motivation comes easily and quickly to me and I am able to motivate others

I am filled with hope and with energy and I live my life fully

I love challenges and I face them head on and win

Motivation is inside of me; I motivate myself

My only option in life is success. I push forward and I succeed

I make a difference to other people and I try to help them to the best of my ability

My ultimate goal is motivation. I only see the goal until I get to it

I know what my worth is and I know that I deserve success; I get success

My work is a true motivator and I will not stop until I achieve my goal

I love life; it is fulfilling and it is beautiful

Chapter 11: Preparing and Using Your Own Affirmations

So, you now know that, if you want to change your beliefs and make a new reality for yourself, you must constantly bombard your mind, conscious and subconscious, with the thoughts of what you truly desire. However, it is very important that you word these thoughts carefully otherwise you may not get the results that you are looking for. As such, there are a number of things that you must do, or not do as the case may be, to get the best result out of your affirmations. I already mentioned some of these earlier but, as with affirmations, it doesn't hurt to repeat things!

- Always do your affirmations in the present tense. The past is gone and cannot be changed. Using the future tense simply tells your mind that you will do something in the future, not that you are doing it now.

Your subconscious mind will always try, very literally, to do what is asked of it. As such, you should say things like, "I am rich", "I have wealth beyond belief", I am ready to be rich and to prosper", or "II choose to be prosperous"

Psychologists say that using the term "choose" is far better because then it becomes your choice. Bear in mind one thing that is very true – what your life is now is as a result of choices that you have made in the past

- Always be positive because only a positive affirmation ill truly work

The subconscious mind struggles to deal with negatives so if you were to say something like, "I am not overweight", by the time it actually reaches your subconscious, the word "not" has been removed or is ignored and that statement turns into "I am overweight".

What really happens comes down to a law we call "Focus and Growth". By this law, whatever you truly focus on will grow. So, when you say to yourself, "I am not overweight", the focus is firmly on "overweight". Your subconscious mind concentrates all its efforts on keeping you or making you overweight so it is far better to say something like, "I am slim and fit" or, "I weigh … kgs/lbs.".

- Positive affirmations can be written down or they can be spoken

When you speak your positive affirmations out loud, say them emphatically, throughout the course of the day. At the very least, what you should be doing is saying each one twenty times every morning, when you get up and then twenty times before you go to bed. This will fix that affirmation into your mind. Even better, say them 100 times a day. The more you can repeat them, the better the result will be.

If you choose to write your affirmations, write each one down at least fifteen times a day. Writing is actually the fastest way to impress something into your subconscious mind. Have you ever heard of Scott Adams? He is a world famous cartoonist, known for "Dilbert" and he is the perfect example of how important written affirmations are. Go find some "Dilbert" and you will see exactly what I mean. Then we have the Mirror technique, which I will tell you more about in a short while.

- Repetition is vital.

If you really want your life to change significantly in any way, your affirmations have to be repeated over and over again through the day. In time, the more you repeat them, they will become a reality to you and not just words. If you were to do them for just a few days, you shouldn't expect to see the results that you want. You have to be like a dog with a bone; keep on going at them until you have achieved your goals.

There is an old story that demonstrates this:

There are two villages, side by side, A and B. Both villages always suffered from a shortage of water. The village called A suddenly discovered a rain dance that they performed and it rained. When they saw this, the village called B also did this rain dance but they never got any rain. They did it a few times, still, no rain fell. In the end, the chief of B went to see the chief of A to ask him for some help. The chief of A simply said to him, "we do this dance until the rains come; we don't do the dance and stop, expecting it to happen"

The same applies to your affirmations – do them and do them continually until you get the result you desire.

The Mirror Technique

One of the best methods for doing positive affirmations is the Mirror Technique and it has been used by many of the greatest authors of self-help books. Here is how to do it:

Stand before your mirror and look deeply into your own eyes. Repeat your affirmations with total gusto and enthusiasm. Fill them with energy. When you look into your own eyes, you will find it much easier to make the connection with your subconscious mind

You must do this regularly. In fact, whenever you are in your own home and you walk past a mirror of any description, stop, look into it, into your eyes and repeat those affirmations several times. This is an incredibly powerful technique and I guarantee you that, done regularly, it will work

The Card Technique

This is another well-known technique and here's how it's done:

Take a piece of card, 3" by 5", or a size that fits into your wallet or your pocket. On it, write your chosen affirmation in large bold lettering. Look at this card frequently throughout the day. It doesn't matter where you are; you can easily whip the card out, read it and then put it back. Don't show it to anyone and don't tell anyone what you are doing because sharing it with others will eliminate all the energy that you have put into the affirmation. Do try and look at the card at least ten times a day, if not more. The more you do it, the more chance there is of your subconscious mind getting to work quicker and bringing about your desires.

Affirmations have been of huge help to thousands upon thousands of people across the world, helping to bring about significant changes, changes that they truly want to happen. But they don't seem to work for everyone so, how can these powerful things bring success for one but fail completely for another?

Affirmations will work to program your subconscious into believing what you are stating. The simple reason for this is, your mind has no idea of the difference between reality and fantasy. When you watch a movie, for example, and you laugh at something or you cry, your mind is actually displaying empathy with the situation and the characters on the screen, even though it isn't real.

There are two types of affirmation – positive and negative. Most of us can, no doubt, go back to our childhoods and can remember being told that we couldn't do something, we didn't have the ability necessary, whether we were told it by a parent, a teacher, even a coach or a friend. They might have told you that were clumsy or fat. These statements stay with you for life. They hide either in your subconscious or conscious mind, and they will be reinforced throughout your entire life – unless you do something to stop them.

According to the Grandfather of Psychology of the Self, Heinz Kohut, fear of failing is more often than not connected to a fear we had in childhood of being abandoned, be it emotionally or physically. When you are afraid of failure, you will automatically overestimate the risks that you are taking and you will always come up with the absolute worst-case scenario. This is the emotional twin of the fear of being abandoned. You will go out of your way to avoid any opportunities that could lead to success and, when you fail, which is inevitable in this case, you are simply reaffirming that negative affirmation, be it something like, "Success will never come to me" or "Success just isn't meant to be in my life".

If that belief has been rooted deeply into your subconscious, it will almost certainly walk all over any positive affirmations, even if you are not really aware of it. This is why positive affirmations don't always work for everyone – their thought patterns have been strongly afflicted by something negative and this is so strong that it can knock away any positives. That said, you can get over this. There are ways to add strength to a positive affirmation so that it can win over the negative. Here we look at a few suggestions on how to make positive affirmations truly work for you:

5 Steps to Making Positive Affirmations More Powerful and Effective
Step 1

Write down in a list everything that you have always considered to be a negative quality of yours. Make sure that you include criticisms that others have made about you, anything that you may have been holding on to. It doesn't matter what it is – it could be something a friend has said to you recently, something your parents, a teacher or a sibling said to you in your childhood or what your boss said to you in your last performance review.

Make sure that you do not, at this stage, judge whether these statements are accurate and do keep in mind that every single person has flaws, whether they believe it or not.

This is one of the simple beauties of being a human being – just write everything down and then look for common threads. It could be something like, "I'm not worthy". This is a great place to begin making changes in your life, positive changes.

When you write down that belief, the one that recurs throughout your statements, take note of whether you are hanging on to that belief within your body. For example, when you write it down, do you get a feeling of dread in your stomach or your heart? A feeling of tightness? If you do, you must now ask yourself if this concept is productive or helpful to your life. If it isn't, ask yourself what would be.

Step 2

Now you have done this, you can write an affirmation that is based on the positive sides of your self-judgment. Have a thesaurus to hand so that you can find truly powerful words that will help boost your affirmations. Instead of writing, for example, "I am worthy", you could write something along the lines of, "I am a remarkable person and I am cherished:".

Once you have written your affirmation down, ask a close friend to read through it and ask them if they have any suggestions that will make your statement stronger

Step 3

When you have your affirmation written exactly as you want it, say it aloud for a minimum of 5 minutes at a time, at least three times per day. Go for first thing in the morning, the middle of the day and last thing at night. The best times are when you are having a shave or applying makeup – look in the mirror, straight into your own eyes, and say the positive affirmation out loud.

You could also write it down a number of times in a notebook as this will help with the reinforcement of that belief into your subconscious. Notice that, as you write it, over the course of time, your writing style will change. This is a big clue as to how your mind is changing, as to how you are perceiving the statement and is a good chart for marking your progression

Step 4

To make sure that your affirmation is firmly anchored in your body, while you are repeating it, put your hand onto the part of your body that felt tight or uncomfortable when you write the negative statement or belief in the first step. For example, if you felt a sinking feeling in your stomach, place your hand over your stomach. Breathe deeply as you say or write your affirmation down. As your mind starts to be reprogrammed, you need to be able to move on from the original concept of that statement to the real and positive feeling of the quality you are looking for.

Step 5

Ask a good friend or a life coach to say your affirmation to you repeatedly. As they are saying, for example, "you are a remarkable person and you are cherished", you must identify that statement as a message that is "good fathering" or "good mothering". If you can't find someone that you trust to help you here, use the mirror technique and use your own reflection to reinforce that message in your mind and body.

Affirmations are incredibly powerful and can help you to change your state of mind, your mood and can help you manifest the changes that you want to bring about in your life. To make them work best, you should first identify the negative belief that is their direct opposite.

If you are finding that these suggestions are still not helping positive affirmations to work for you, it may be that you have deep-seated fears and irrationals that can only be dealt with through the help of a professionally trained therapist. It could be that you are not consciously aware of what it is, it could be buried deeply in your subconscious and must be uncovered if this is to work for you.

Mindfulness meditation is a fantastic tool that can help you to unbury unhealthy thought patterns and helps you to put them into categories, allowing you to properly identify these that are positive and those that are negative or afflicted. Mindfulness is not about changing you; it is about having the power to accept what is and then change to what is possible

Conclusion

Congratulations, you have made it to the end of this book. I hope that as you have read this book, you have found quotes and affirmations that have caused you to dig deep into yourself and find the potential buried inside. Now that you have set the foundation and begun changing your mindset, you are ready to take what you have learned and fill your life with happiness, success, and optimism.

As you move forward, remember to continue saying the affirmations that you feel speak to you the loudest. You don't want to say thirty plus affirmations a day, but choose the ones that most apply to your life and continue saying them on a daily basis. Saying affirmations every day has the power to bring great things into your life. Think about all of the ways that your life has improved in the last thirty days. You are no longer the person who picked his book up a month ago. You are now more confident and ready to take on the world.

Thank you again for downloading my book, "*Positive Thinking: 30 Days Of Motivation And Affirmations: Change Your "Mindset" & Fill Your Life With Happiness, Success, & Optimism!*" I hope you enjoyed the readings in this book and wish you all the best on your continuing journey.

Help me improve this book

While I have never met you, if you made it through this book I know that you are the kind of person that is wanting to get better and is willing to take on tough feedback to get to that point. You and I are cut from the same cloth in that respect. I am always looking to get better and I wish to not just improve myself, but also this book. If you have positive feedback, please take the time to leave a review. It will help other find this book and it can help change a life in the same way that it changed yours. If you have constructive feedback, please also leave a review. It will help me better understand what you, the reader, need to make significant improvements in your life. I will take your feedback and use it to improve this book so that it can become more powerful and beneficial to all those who come in contact with it.

Free Special Report

If you are interested in taking your life to the next level Mastermind Self Development has an amazing offer for you. For a limited time, we are offering a FREE special report on the Wheel of Life. This report will give you a visual look at your current life and then take you through a series of exercises that will help you plan out what a perfect life looks life for you. The workbook does not end there; we then take you through a process to help you plan out how to achieve that perfect life. The process is very powerful and has the potential to change your life forever. Take advantage of it now by going to our website www.mastermindselfdevelopment.com/specialreport

www.ingramcontent.com/pod-product-compliance
Lightning Source LLC
Chambersburg PA
CBHW081359070526
44583CB00020B/2601